TIMES OF GRACE

ROGER POELMAN

TIMES OF GRACE

The Sign of Forty

in the Bible

HERDER AND HERDER

1964
HERDER AND HERDER NEW YORK
232 Madison Avenue, New York 16, New York

Translated from *Le signe biblique des quarante jours*
(Paris: Éditions Universitaires, 1961) by D. P. Farina.

Nihil Obstat: Paul Couture, S.S.E.
Censor Librorum Delegatus

Imprimatur: Patrick C. Brennan
Vicar General of Burlington
December 3, 1963

Library of Congress Catalog Card Number 64–13689
© 1964 by Herder and Herder, Incorporated
Printed in the United States of America

CONTENTS

5

The biblical passages quoted in the course of this work are based upon the Douay-Rheims version of the Bible, with frequent modifications incorporating the renderings of the French version of the Bible of Jerusalem.

The name *Yahweh* has been replaced with *Everlasting* (in French, *Éternel*). This, we admit, is a very inadequate word and not so expressive as its Hebrew equivalent; but how else to emphasize the fact that we are dealing with a personal name—the name of God, who has revealed himself and appeared to Moses? We might have employed the name *Lord* as do the Masoretic text, the Septuagint, and the Vulgate. Unfortunately, this word has lost too much of its original meaning for us moderns.

Preface

All these things befell them as a type, but they were written as a warning to us.—1 Cor 10:11.

THE contemporary movement in biblical studies has been most successful in historical and critical investigation. Theological studies have not failed to appear; but most of these studies have been written within the limited circle of professional interpreters, and many observers have expressed disappointment that the theological results of historical and critical studies have not been made known sufficiently to a wider and deeply interested public. One area of theological interpretation which has been neglected is typology. Typological interpretation, original in the Bible itself and very frequently employed by the Fathers of the Church, lapsed into uncontrolled fancy during the Middle Ages and the centuries which followed; and contemporary interpreters generally have not attempted it. Several writers have suggested a revival of typology according to the spirit and method of the Fathers of the Church; but it is difficult to combine these methods with the principles and practice of contemporary interpretation, and the revival of patristic interpretation has not been received with enthusiasm by students of the Bible.

M. Poelman is one of a group of writers who have approached typology from the established principles of modern interpretation. In this book he studies what might appear to be at first glance a purely coincidental collection of passages grouped about a theme which might appear trivial: the events which are connected with a period of forty days or forty years. The theme of forty arises from a consideration of the forty days of Lent, an obvious liturgical echo of the forty days of Jesus in the desert. The forty-day sojourn of Jesus, in turn, echoes a number of Old Testament episodes, which M. Poelman assembles. Far from being merely coincidental, the themes come together in a theological symphony. Sin, judgment and grace recur in each of them; and the sign of forty becomes a sign of crisis—a Greek word which means judgment.

M. Poelman's approach is bold; indeed, some will think it rash. But it is a proof of the courage and the integrity of a writer that he is willing to venture into the areas of unproved hypotheses. Advance in understanding is impossible if one assures oneself that he treads on no ground which others have not trodden before him. At the same time, the explorer needs some assurance that he is moving in the right direction. This assurance is furnished here by the basic principle of all biblical typology, that Jesus is the new Israel and that the new Israel lives on in the Church. The person and mission of Jesus are conceived and presented in the New Testament in this manner more frequently than we have yet fully discovered. Obscure details become meaningful when it is recognized that the New Testament writers have seen in these details a community between the Gospel event and the Israel event. A pattern emerges in these details, never expressly set forth as such; and this pattern is the knowledge of the God who reveals, who acts and who saves. The writers of the New Testament were sure that Jesus is not recognized in his true identity unless he is recognized as the new Israel who fulfills the destiny of the people of God's election. Typology cannot be omitted if one wishes to see the full reality of the Incarnate Word.

M. Poelman's book will introduce to the English-speaking public a type of exposition which has not yet been done extensively by writers whose native tongue is English. It is my personal conviction that their understanding of the Bible and of contemporary studies will be enriched by such works, which have been well received in Europe by the general public to whom they are addressed.

JOHN L. MCKENZIE, S.J.

Introduction

THE biblical narrative of prehistoric events contains an account of the Deluge. The Deluge lasted forty days and forty nights. This number is a symbolic, not a mathematical, expression. What reality does it symbolize?

Moses spent two forty-day periods on Mount Horeb or Sinai. This sojourn, too, is placed in a particular perspective. Is it connected with that of the Deluge?

When Elias went to Mount Sinai to meet the Lord and renew his vocation, his journey, we are told in the Book of Kings, took forty days and forty nights.

And did the period of penance and grace announced by Jonas to Babylon not contain characteristic features justifying its duration of forty days?

Finally, when it is no longer a question of one man but of the vocation of a whole people—God's People—the symbolism persists, except that here the forty days becomes forty years in the desert. Who would not be struck by the recurrence of this number?

At the beginning of his public life, Jesus, Our Lord, was baptized in the Jordan. Before he did anything else, "led by the Holy Spirit" he retired to the mountain in the desert of Karantal, and there remained forty days and forty nights.

And after Christ rose from the dead, the Gospels report one final delay of forty days before he ascended into Heaven. Certainly the Evangelists have taken up this scriptural problem in the teaching of God.

If we can glimpse the meaning of all this, we shall undoubtedly come to a better understanding of the reasons the Church has for proposing to Christians a forty-day period of Lent.

The forty days of the Deluge ended with God's covenant with Noah, just as the forty days of Moses and the forty years of the People terminated with the Covenant of Sinai.

The forty days Christ spent in the desert were a prelude to the new and eternal Covenant of the Pasch, just as the forty days of the risen Christ on earth were a prelude to his taking up his post in Heaven as sole mediator between God and men.

Elias' forty days were intended to refresh his prophetic soul at the very source of the Mosaic alliance, while in Jonas' case they extended the benefits of grace to pagan Nineveh.

In like manner the Church's Lent prepares man for the renewal of the final Alliance during the Easter vigil.

All who have been regenerated in the waters of baptism, purified of all their sins, and strengthened by the manna of the Eucharist can begin their journey in newness of life toward the mountain where God appears.

The Forty Days of the Deluge

And the Deluge fell upon the earth forty days and forty nights.
[Gn 7:12]

THE first chapters of Genesis convey theological realities and revealed truths by means of imagery and traditional lore from various sources mostly originating in Mesopotamia and neighboring regions.

What the exact background is of these images and ideas is difficult to say. What can be said, however, is that the biblical writer selected them, purified them, and left the seal of his own individuality on them. Through them he teaches us the truths of God's revelation.

Such is the story of Cain and Abel and that of the Tower of Babel.

Such also is the story of the Deluge.

About the latter, exegetes have discovered several traditions mingled together in the sacred texts. One of them is the Yahwist tradition, so called from the Hebrew name *Yahweh,* by which it designates God. This tradition was kept alive in the stories told in the patriarchal tents of Canaan; it came down from father to son in the land of Gessen, by the Nile, for five long centuries; it was retold in the Sinai Desert during the forty years' migration and enlivened the long encampments at oases.

One day an anonymous writer thought of collecting the details of this tradition and committing them to writing. This happened about 800 B.C., when the two kingdoms of Judah and Israel were separating. Our Yahwist lived in the southern kingdom of Judah,

13

close to Jerusalem. His account is characterized by a simple and fresh artlessness. Practical, introspective, and descriptive, he looked on all things, so to speak, against the background of Yahweh, the Lord, or Everlasting, as we awkwardly render the Hebrew word. His whole outlook was religious and at the same time very human; in human history he read the history of God's grace.

The contribution to the biblical narrative of this anonymous author is difficult to separate from that of another writer, who lived in the northern kingdom, Israel. He too sat down, a little later, to compose a history of the beginnings of the world. To distinguish him from the former, biblical scholars call him the Elohist, from the Hebrew name *Elohim,* by which he calls God.

The Elohist has a style and views of his own. He does not go back so far as the Yahwist (he does not mention the Deluge, for instance), but in a way he is more theological-minded, and his style is more solemn.

His writings found their way to Jerusalem, carried thither by refugees from the north when in 722 B.C. the kingdom of Israel collapsed. The two traditions thus became so intertwined that we never find them independent from each other. For this reason, scriptural scholars' conjectures on the identity of either ought to be advanced with caution. Yet the single revealed message is clarified by the convergence of these two sources, much as the contours of a statue are thrown into sharper relief by the light of several hidden spots.

Besides these two writers, there is a third source for the Genesis narrative—the Priestly source, which is of special value for the story of the Deluge.

Let us remember that the great turning point in the religious history of the People of God occurred during the Exile. When

God's People were taken in chains to Babylon in 587 B.C., they had lost everything—country, king, and temple. The last terrible sight the captives had had of Jerusalem was the devouring fire that destroyed the city and turned to ashes the only temple on earth built to the true God.

Furthermore, the Jews in exile no longer had organized worship. Was this, then, to be the end of everything? Indeed not. An extraordinary religious reorganization and vitalization took place. The Jews began those meetings for prayer and instruction that came to be called synagogues, that is, assemblies. The People were recreated, as it were, by the word of God.

The Chosen People had taken with them to Babylon all their sacred writings, and there, during the Exile, God raised in their midst great religious leaders—the prophets of the Captivity— especially the author of the second book of Isaias (chaps. 40–45) and the priest-prophet Ezechiel. These leaders wrote commentaries on the history of the past intended to explain the present and sustain hope in the future. There was also the group of "priests" who had come to Babylon with the People. They too commented on, read, preserved, and copied the sacred Scriptures. During this period there was a great deal of transcribing, revising, arranging, and rethinking of these ancient texts, which truly preserved the unity of the People in exile.

Thus, during the Captivity and for a little while after the Jews' re-entry into Palestine, the finishing touches were added to what has been called the Priestly Code. Collecting and arranging old written traditions, these priest-writers compiled the Book of Leviticus and touched up ("edited," we would say today) the Books of Numbers, Exodus, and Genesis. We can identify the influence of these Priests mingled with that of the Yahwist in the episodes of the Deluge.

THE RELIGIOUS MESSAGE OF THE DELUGE

In the Bible as it has come down to us through these various sources, what is the religious message which the account of the forty-day Deluge is intended to convey to us?

Everlasting saw that the wickedness of men was great upon earth and that all the thought of their heart was bent upon evil at all times.

Everlasting regretted that he had made man on the earth and was grieved to the heart. Then Everlasting said, "I will wipe from the surface of the earth man whom I have created—man and beast, crawling creatures and the birds of the air—for I regret that I made them."

But Noah found favor in the eyes of Everlasting. [Gn 6:5–8]

Alas! The first enlightenment reveals the corruption of man. This religious reality is of fundamental importance if we would understand how man really stands before God.

We have already been told of Adam's sin and of the first human death at Cain's hands; and now we are told that man's increasing civilization has become more and more corrupt. Indeed, the heart of man is bent upon evil at all times; God's creation of free men seems to have been an utter failure. And this failure is supremely important to God.

The simple, anthropomorphic terms used by the writer prove to be very forceful when we analyze them. Everlasting regrets having created man—and the text is insistent: "man whom I have created." God who made man after his own image out of pure love is now going to have to destroy him. But what a revelation appears in that last verse: "But Noah found favor in the eyes of Everlasting." There is someone, then, who has stood loyal, someone who has earned God's favor, a remnant of humanity, a sapling that can still be replanted. That is the message.

The old Yahwist narrative describes here the plan involving

Noah. A flood sent by God will cover the earth so that a fresh start may be made. Noah is to construct an ark according to God's specifications, and the length and breadth and height of it are symbols of God's protection and loving wisdom. During the upheaval Noah and his family and representatives of the first creation—the "remnant"—will be in God's keeping. The narrative continues:

Then Everlasting said to Noah, "Go into the ark, you and all your household, for only you, in this generation, I have found just in my sight. . . .

"For . . . after seven days I will send rain on the earth for forty days and forty nights, and I will wipe from the surface of the earth every living thing that I have made."

And Noah did all that Everlasting commanded him. [Gn 7:1, 4–5]

One final respite is allowed by God's patience, and then comes the scourge, frightful and devastating for sinners, while Noah, the just man who will make a new beginning possible, is saved. This is how sacred Scripture views and explains the Deluge, a theme already popular in ancient Babylonian accounts.

To God's command, Noah replies not with words but with prompt action. "Noah did all that Everlasting commanded him, and Everlasting shut him in on the outside" (Gn 7:16b). This sentence is arresting in its simplicity: God's grace is overwhelming, and there is nothing to do but abandon oneself to it. And here we enter into the famous biblical period of the forty days. In it two aspects are simultaneously emphasized—chastisement and grace.

[On that day] all the sources of the great deep and the floodgates of heaven were opened.[1] And the Deluge fell upon the earth forty days and forty nights. [Gn 7:11–12]

[1] "The waters from below and those from above broke down the dikes God had built to contain them (Gn 1:7); it is a return to chaos." This is a note of the Bible of Jerusalem.

And further on:

And the Deluge continued forty days upon the earth. The waters increased and bore up the ark, and it rose above the earth. . . .

All that were on dry land in whose nostrils was the breath of life, died. And Everlasting wiped out every living thing on the earth, from man to beast, crawling creatures and the birds of the air: they were wiped out from the earth. Only Noah and those with him in the ark were left. [Gn 7:17, 22–23]

God's judgment is seen not only in this total destruction but also in the survival of the "just man" and, because of him, of those who are with him. For at the end of this long "quarantine," "God remembered Noah and all the beasts that were with him in the ark." This "remembrance" by God points immediately to grace: if God remembers, everything is well, everything is at peace.

The narrative continues in its appealing simplicity:

At the end of forty days, Noah opened the window which he had made in the ark and released a raven. It flew to and from until the waters had dried off the earth. Then he sent a dove to see if the waters had abated from the surface of the ground. But the dove found no place to alight. So she returned to him in the ark, for the waters covered the whole earth. He put forth his hand and caught her and drew her to him in the ark.

He waited another seven days and again sent forth the dove from the ark. The dove came back to him in the evening, and there in her mouth was a green olive leaf.

So Noah knew that the waters had abated from the earth. Then he waited another seven days and sent forth the dove. But she did not return to him any more.

. . . Noah removed the covering of the ark and saw that the surface of the ground had dried. [Gn 8:6–12, 13b]

This picturesque account that charmed our childhood is unforgettable. But what is the revealed truth it enfolds? This, after all, is what we must look for in the Bible. "After seven days I will send rain on the earth," the narrative ran before the Deluge; and now again seven days elapse after the devastation. These seven-day periods seem to isolate all the better the forty-day upheaval; they signify one last delay.

Like a navigator bent on discovery, Noah releases the dove to see if land is near. The returning messenger with an olive branch in its beak symbolizes the restoration of peace and salvation. Everything is green, everything is possible again! Noah then unlatches the roof of the ark and scans the horizon: land!

When he climbs out of the ark with the group of beings saved by God's pure grace, Noah appears as a new Adam. And the first construction in this new creation is an altar, the first action a sacrifice.

Noah built an altar to Everlasting, took of every clean animal, and offered holocausts on the altar. When Everlasting smelled the sweet odor he said to himself, "I will never again curse the ground." [Gn 8:20–21]

What joy! God accepts the burnt offering; it pleases him, he finds it an agreeable odor!

At that moment we hear the strains of a chant that must be very ancient, whose theme Jeremias (Jer 5:24) as well as St. Paul (Acts 14:17) will again take up—the chant of creation in the cycle of its seasons: "As long as the earth shall last, seedtime and harvest, cold and heat, summer and winter, day and night shall not cease" (Gn 8:22).

Upon this altar and amid the fumes of this sacrifice is born the divine idea of a covenant.

A covenant! God wishes to be with men, to cast his lot, so to say, with them. From the beginning, this alliance is conceived as a nuptial union, "for your spouse is your creator" (Is 54:5):

Then God said to Noah and to his sons with him: "I will establish my covenant with you and with your descendants after you and with every living creature that is with you, the birds, the cattle, and every wild animal with you, all that came out of the ark. . . .

"I will establish my covenant with you: never again will all flesh be destroyed by the waters of the flood; never again will there be a flood to destroy the earth."

And God said: "This is the token of the covenant; I set it between me and you and every living creature that is with you, for all generations to come: I will set my bow in the clouds and it shall be a token of the covenant between me and the earth." [Gn 9:8–13]

It is to be observed that in these recollections of primordial history concerning the forty-day Deluge and its salutary effects, no particular human people is mentioned. God's covenant with Noah is intended for all creatures: it is universal.

Did we perhaps suppose that human iniquity had offended God irremediably, or that the waters of the Deluge had drowned his love? "Stern as death is love. . . . Deep waters cannot quench love, nor floods sweep it away" (Ct 8:6–7).

The rainbow is a symbol of God's choosing, like oil and water, like fire and bread. It sparkles with every color in creation. It marks the dawn of a new era of forgiveness and peace.

When in the Apocalypse St. John has a vision of heaven, the first thing he describes is a throne—the throne of God. Before the throne is a sea of glass, similar to crystal, "and there was a rainbow around about the throne, in appearance like to an emerald" (Ap 4:2–6). In heaven's grand liturgy we are told of this area of mercy and peace around the throne of God. Further on John describes the arrival of an angel, one of the fairest in the Apocalypse:

And I saw another angel, a strong one, coming down from heaven, clothed in a cloud, and the rainbow was over his head, and his face was like the sun, and his feet like pillars of fire.

And he had in his hand a little open scroll; and he set his right foot upon the sea, but his left upon the earth . . . and he lifted up his hand to heaven, and swore by him who lives forever and ever, who created heaven and the things that are therein, and the earth and the things that are therein, and the sea and the things that are therein, that there shall be delay no longer.

But in the days of the voice of the seventh angel, when he begins to sound the trumpet, the mystery of God will be accomplished, as he declared by his servants the prophets. [Ap 10:1–7]

The rainbow of Genesis announces God's mercy upon primeval creation—sowings and reapings, days and nights. This apocalyptic angel, haloed in the mystery of mercy and peace for all saved souls, announces the end of time. He takes possession of creation, planting one foot on the sea and another on the earth and pointing his finger to the sky, announcing that time will be no more, that God's mystery is about to be consummated: "And I saw a new heaven and a new earth; for the first heaven and the first earth had passed away, and the sea was no more" (Ap 21:1). The holy city, the new Jerusalem, can now descend from God's throne in heaven, as a new bride.

NEW TESTAMENT COMMENT ON THE MEANING OF THE DELUGE

The patience of God waited in the days of Noah, while the ark was building. [1 Pt 3:20]

There is a time of respite, then, but let there be no mistake: the time for justice will surely come. The author of the Epistle to

the Hebrews and Christ himself testify to this theological trait of
the Genesis narrative.

By faith Noah, having been warned concerning things not seen as yet,
prepared with pious fear an ark in which to save his household. By
faith, having thus condemned the world, he was made heir of the
justice. [Heb. 11:7]

We have here a typical example of one Scripture passage
interpreting another. The Epistle to the Hebrews introduces us
to the symbolism of Genesis: everything is seen in reference to the
mystery of faith and salvation, fear and justice. Thus, Scripture
yields its own mature fruit and operates within its own proper
field; Scripture is the book of God and man.

Here is the authority of Jesus Christ himself:

In the days before the flood they were eating and drinking, marrying
and giving in marriage, until the day when Noah entered the ark, and
they did not understand until the flood came and swept them all
away; even so will be the coming of the Son of man. [Mt 24:37–38]

Jesus warns us here that the theology of prehistoric times is
symbolic and typological, and points out what our attitude ought
to be: "Watch, therefore, for you know not at what hour your
Lord is to come." Such is the message that recurs in all the eschatological parables having reference to the passage we have quoted.
Is is obvious that the Deluge is for Christ something other than
a simple example, than a comparison drawn from a fund of
images. He sees in it, as St. John calls it, the consummation of
God's mystery.

Such too was the view of the first Gospel preachers.

This first thing you must know is that in the last days there will come
deceitful scoffers, men walking according to their own lusts, saying,
"Where is the promise of his coming? For since the fathers fell asleep,
all things continue as they were from the beginning of creation."

22

For of this they are willfully ignorant, that there were heavens long ago and an earth formed out of water and by water through the word of God; and that by these means the world that then was perished, deluged with water.

But the heavens that now are and the earth, by that same word have been stored up, being reserved for fire against the day of judgment and destruction of ungodly men.

But, beloved, do not be ignorant of this one thing, that one day with the Lord is as a thousand years, and a thousand years as one day. [2 Pt 3:3–8]

The author of this second Epistle of St. Peter portrays the end of the world by fire as the final resumption of that first purification by water. The same realities are involved: sin, grace, judgment.

Thus the Old Testament foreshadows the realities of the New, and the New Testament in turn introduces us to the eternal realities "by inaugurating them."

A thousand years are as a day with God. No temporal quantity is involved here, but rather a time quality: we are at the end of the world. The Christian soul lives in the imminence of Christ's return. The idea of a delay—a respite given by God—is constant throughout history. How many centuries had to elapse before the first Christmas! But one day the Word was made flesh and pitched his tent among us. *In the same manner* the risen Christ will appear in his glory one day. The Church's whole existence is orientated toward that day.

The Lord does not delay in his promises, as certain men accuse him of delay, but for your sake he is long-suffering, not wishing that any should perish but that all should turn to repentance.

But the day of the Lord will come as a thief; at that time the heavens will pass away with great violence, and the elements will be dissolved with heat, and the earth and the works that are in it will be burnt up.

Seeing therefore that all these things are to be dissolved, what manner of men ought you to be in holy and pious behavior, awaiting and hastening the coming of the day of God? [2 Pt 3:9–12]

Texts such as this are full of religious significance. They reveal an interest, a concern with that mystery of resurrection and life beyond the grave. And this makes it all the more important for us not to delete a single word of God, but to accept them all with respect, prudence, and eagerness even when we cannot integrate them into our own favorite theory. The last words of the passage just quoted give the purpose of this first Lenten message: how holy should your life be! And the note of hope heard in the final sentence of this Epistle is sounded with equal emphasis in St. John's Apocalypse (21:1): "We look for new heavens and a new earth" (2 Pt 3:13).

God has made things so that they might exist. In this present creation we are already brushing shoulders with what will rise to a permanent life in the world to come.

After the Deluge, creation made a fresh start. Issuing forth from the ark, Noah had the promise of the same divine blessings that had already been pronounced in the garden of Eden.[2] But after this final purification we shall again find the river of life, the tree of life, the fruits of life, but chiefly the intimate vision of God: "And his servants will adore him; and they will see his face, and his name will be on their foreheads" (Ap 22:4).

This yearning desire that throbs in the final words of the Apocalypse is then easy to understand:

And [the angel] said to me, "These words are trustworthy and true; and the Lord, the God who inspires the prophets, sent his angel to show to his servants what must shortly come to pass—and behold, I come quickly! . . ."

[2] See Gn 8:15, 19; and 9:1, 11.

24

And the Spirit and the bride [the Spirit in the Church, through her mouth] say: "Come!" And let him who hears say: "Come!" . . .

Amen! Come, Lord Jesus! [Ap 22:6–7, 17, 20]

This first biblical forty-day period, we may say in conclusion, deals with a time replete with divine activity—a chastisement by water and a salvation by grace. It emphasizes hope: hope and patient expectation. It climaxes in the covenant between God and Noah concerning the whole world.

The Forty-Day Periods of Moses

At the end of the forty days and forty nights, Everlasting gave me the tablets of the covenant. [Dt 9:11]

THE FIRST FORTY–DAY PERIOD

THE first biblical quarantine ended with God's covenant with Noah. The second and the third bring in the Mosaic alliance.

Impressively majestic, these periods are appropriately portrayed against the background of the Sinai: deep-scarred cliffs, red-tinted with porphyry, with layers here and there of black basalt and yellow schist.

Austere and solitary, the top of Djebel Mousa (Moses' Mountain), 7500 feet above sea level, looks out over a magnificent panorama. This is the place, according to tradition, where the two forty-day periods of Moses passed.

Everlasting has delivered his People from Egypt, carried them, as it were, on eagle wings across the desert and brought them into his presence to be made into a priestly kingdom and a consecrated race. The time of the Covenant is now come, and God is about to promulgate its text. The crowd is encamped at Er Raha, a vast plain surrounded by a high wall of ragged cliffs. God summons Moses to the mountain of Horeb-Sinai.

. . . a cloud covered the mountain. And the glory of Everlasting dwelt upon Sinai, covering it with a cloud six days.

On the seventh day Everlasting called to Moses out of the midst of the cloud.

And the sight of the glory of Everlasting was like a burning fire upon the top of the mountain, in the eyes of the children of Israel.

And Moses, entering into the midst of the cloud, went up into the mountain; and he was there forty days and forty nights. [Ex 24:15–18]

The way the text presents the episode is very significant.[1] First, there is the background of the mountain enveloped by clouds and the devouring fire on its summit. Cloud and fire are like tokens of God's glory, feeble indications to human senses of God's transcendence when he reveals himself to men. Glory is the divine attribute that men can apprehend. Further, such words— cloud, fire, glory—have a history of their own throughout the Bible, from the Old to the New Testament, right up to the Apocalypse.

Moses ventures into the cloud on God's summons (no one would dare do so on his own!) and remains on the mountain forty days and forty nights. There he is, a man plunged in the mystery of God's presence. The meeting defies description. Mystics have at times attempted an account of their meetings with God, but none of their roles were so important as that of this man, Moses.

The first constituent of this forty-day retreat we notice is the fast: "I stayed on the mountain forty days and forty nights without eating or drinking" (Dt 9:9). What is there to sustain Moses? ("I have food to eat of which you do not know" [Jn 4:32]). The life-giving word of God.

Moses is the man of God's word. The final redaction of Exodus, aiming as it does at presenting the development of Israel's political and religious institutions as the very expression of God's will,

---

[1] The Ex passages quoted in this chapter are of various origins—mostly Yahwist and Elohist. Two passages are from the Priestly Code, 24:15–18 and 34:29–35.

links up such institutions with Moses on the summit of Sinai. The first verse of chapter 25 begins: "And Everlasting spoke to Moses, saying," and chapter 31 ends: "When Everlasting had ended these words on Mount Sinai, he gave to Moses two stone tablets of testimony, written with the finger of God." Fasting and prayer dispose man to the reception of God's word. Moses' real hunger is a hunger for God.

Stone tablets written with the finger of God—the living pen God uses to write with is Moses himself. The writing on these tablets is none other than God's inspired Scriptures.

And these Ten Words, or as we call them these Ten Commandments, what are they? What do they convey to us? They do not contain a divine fantasy, the arbitrary decrees of an all-powerful tyrant; they convey to us a precious and extraordinary gift, the gift of a good and provident Father to the children of his predilection. It is as if God had said: "My children, my People, I who alone understand man whom I have made to my own image and likeness come to point out to you the path that does not stray, the tenfold path of love."

When Jesus was asked: "Master, what is the great commandment of the Law?" his prompt answer was like a wave surging up from the depths and invading his heart: "The first and the greatest commandment is this: you shall love the Lord your God with your whole heart and with your whole soul and with your whole mind. This is the greatest and the first commandment. And the second is like it: you shall love your neighbor as yourself." And he added, thus giving us an explanation of the whole Old Testament, especially of the Ten Words: "On these two commandments depend the whole law and the prophets" (Mt 22:35–40).

Such are the Ten Words, written by God's finger on the tablets which Moses brings back from the mountain.

The Golden Calf

But alas! While Moses converses with God during the first forty days, the People of divine choice and predilection, the race consecrated to God, "return in their hearts to Egypt," as the Bible expressively puts it. They eat, drink, and chant around the idol they have set up and offer sacrilegious sacrifice to the golden calf. The contrast between the mystery consummated on Sinai and the insane revelry of the plain is revolting.

When the people became aware of Moses' delay in coming down from the mountain, they gathered around Aaron and said to him: "Come! make us a god who will be our leader. As for the man Moses who brought us out of the land of Egypt, we do not know what has happened to him."

Aaron replied: "Have your wives and sons and daughters take off the golden earrings they are wearing and bring them to me."

So the people took off their earrings and brought them to Aaron, who accepted their offerings, and, fashioning this gold with a graving tool, made a golden calf.

Then they cried out: "This is thy god, O Israel, who brought you out of the land of Egypt."

On seeing this, Aaron built an altar before the calf and proclaimed: "Tomorrow is a feast of Yahweh."

Early the next day, the people offered holocausts and brought peace offerings. Then they sat down to eat and drink and rose up to revel. [Ex 32:1–6]

What is the meaning of this passage? It describes a distortion of the true religion. It does not mean that the Jews somehow are rebelling against God; it rather suggests an attempt to "material-ize" him, to establish a sort of ownership over him, to bring him within their reach. They fret over the delay; they have no patience. They take the initiative, and want to determine the course of events themselves. "Come! make us a god who will be our leader." And of course Moses, God's ambassador, is entirely forgotten. "The disciple is not above his master."

The saddest figure in the whole affair is perhaps Aaron. Aaron is Moses' brother and the future high priest. To fashion a god you need gold.[2] The Jews remember the Egyptian idols—Apis, the bull god—and the processions and the revels. What an insult to offer God! What a return for his love, just when he is giving his commandments, just when he is revealing himself and seeking man's love! And this liturgical parody, too! Alas, the holiest things become the most abject when it is no longer God who guides.

God informs Moses on his mountain retreat of what is happening:

Everlasting said to Moses: "Come! Go down at once to your people whom you brought out of the land of Egypt, for they have become depraved. They have soon turned aside from the way I pointed out to them, making for themselves a molten calf and worshiping it, sacrificing to it and crying out: 'This is your god, O Israel, who brought you out of the land of Egypt.'" [Ex 32:7–8]

All this passage is very human in the way it is presented; it is also very skillfully written, revealing as it does an inner conflict in Moses. Note the word *you* in God's speech: ". . . your people whom you brought out of the land of Egypt." We witness here an attempt to dissociate Moses, whom God proposes to make the father of another race, from the people whom God intends to reject:

"I see how stiff-necked this people is," continued Everlasting to Moses. "Let me alone, then, that my wrath may blaze up against them and

[2] There is no question here of the worship of money (mammon), as is often suggested. On the contrary, the people have been generous. It is idolatry, a sin against the true religion, that is hateful.

consume them. Then I will make of you a great nation." [Ex 32:9–10]

But Moses will never abandon his people. His spiritual outlook is that of a shepherd: he lives for his flock and will never let himself be parted from it. He will share in its fate to the end, and will end by saving it. In this, is Moses not exactly like Jesus, an image of the mediator of the New Covenant? Moses was his people's intermediary at the time of the plagues of Egypt; he will remain their intercessor throughout their sojourn in the desert. Listen to how he expostulates with God, how he foresees the Egyptians gloating over the downfall of the Chosen People, but above all how he reminds God of his promises:

Moses implored Everlasting, his God, saying: "Why, O Everlasting, should your wrath blaze up against your own people whom you brought out of the land of Egypt with such great power and with so strong a hand? Why should the Egyptians say: 'With evil intent he brought them out, that he might kill them in the mountains and exterminate them from the face of the earth'? Let your blazing wrath die down! Relent in punishing your people!

"Remember your servants Abraham, Isaac, and Israel, and how you swore to them by your own self, saying: 'I will make your descendants as numerous as the stars of the sky, and all this land that I promised I will give your descendants as their perpetual inheritance.'" [Ex 32:11–13]

"*Your* people," God says to Moses. "*Your* people," insists Moses to God, recalling his wonders and solemn pledges. It is just the right way to go about it—to remind God of his love. Exodus concludes this passage by remarking, "Everlasting was appeased from doing the evil which he had spoken against his people." Face to face with his People, God relents and "shows mercy."

Moses has turned to God and the essential has been obtained. He turns now to the people. A prophet, he must show Israel the

31

heinousness of their sin, must show them that they deserve to die for breaking the Covenant.

Moses then turned and came down the mountain with the two tablets of the Commandments in his hands: tablets that were written on both sides, front and back; tablets that were made by God, having inscriptions on them that were engraved by God himself. [Ex 32:15–16]

Josue has now joined Moses. Coming close to the camp, they hear shouts, and Josue fears a battle has broken out; but Moses notices that the noise proceeds from alternate choruses. The camp is reveling in unbridled frenzy, in the drunken cult of the golden calf.

As he drew near the camp, he saw the calf and the dancing. With that Moses' wrath flared up so that he threw the tablets down and broke them on the base of the mountain. [Ex 32:19]

One is reminded of God's words before the Deluge: "I will wipe from the surface of the earth man whom I have created" (Gn 6:7). This is the reaction of disappointed love. Moses seizes the precious tablets carrying the foundation of the divine Covenant and dashes them to pieces. Let the People understand this prophetic outburst!

The golden calf is burned and ground to dust. This dust Moses orders to be mixed with water and given as a drink to the children of Israel, thus emphasizing their participation in the general apostasy. Let them all swallow their sin, let it cling to their entrails! Atonement is achieved through a ruthless purification of blood. After this, the shepherd, reunited with his flock, resumes with them his journey toward the Lord.

On the next day Moses said to his people: "You have committed a great sin. I will go up to Everlasting now. Perhaps I may be able to make atonement for your sin." So Moses went back to Everlasting and said:

"Alas! this people has indeed committed a grave sin by making a god of gold for themselves. If you would but forgive their sin . . . ! If you will not, then strike me out of the book that you have written." [Ex 32:30–32]

One is reminded of St. Paul, explaining his feeling of solidarity with the men of his race and revealing his sadness and love:

I speak the truth in Christ: I do not lie, my conscience bearing me witness in the Holy Spirit that I have great sadness and continuous sorrow in my heart. For I could wish to be anathema myself from Christ for the sake of my brethren who are my kinsmen according to the flesh; who are Israelites, who have the adoption as sons, and the glory, and the covenants, and the legislation, and the worship, and the promises; who have the fathers, and from whom is the Christ according to the flesh, who is, over all things, God blessed forever! Amen. [Rom 9:1–5]

The Meeting Tent

At this point in Exodus, we come across a few verses forming a short narrative which has come down to us from a different tradition but which is very suggestive and closely related in its implications to the episode of the golden calf:

The Tent, which was called the Meeting Tent, Moses used to pitch at some distance away, outside the camp.

Anyone who wished to consult Everlasting would go to this Meeting Tent outside the camp.

Whenever Moses would go to the Tent, the people would all arise and stand at the entrance of their own tents, watching Moses until he entered the Tent. As Moses entered the Tent the column of cloud would come down and stand at its entrance, while Everlasting spoke with Moses.

On seeing the column of cloud stand at the entrance of the Tent, all the people would rise and worship at the entrance of their own tents.

Everlasting spoke to Moses face to face as a man is wont to speak to his friend. [Ex 33:7–11]

We have here, then, a special kind of tent, a tent that at present serves the same purpose that the Temple will serve one day. It is the dwelling of God. Here the People can communicate with God through their mediator, Moses. But is it not really because of the man who enters it and of him who resides in it that it is given the very significant name *Meeting Tent?* What meeting? The meeting of God and Moses.

After the idolatry of the golden calf, in a gesture that is at the same time mysterious and allusive like a parable, Moses pitches this Tent at a good distance from the camp, which is thus excommunicated from God. After all, hadn't the People broken the Covenant?

Each visit of Moses to the Tent is like a roll call of the People. The text conjures up the reverence and religious fear which the event arouses among them. They silently assemble before the entrances of their tents and follow with their eyes the man of God. As Moses enters the Tent, a column of cloud appears before the entrance. In the tradition of the Bible, the cloud represents the boundary between the visible and the invisible world whenever God appears and wherever God dwells.

Everlasting, then, confers with Moses. It is he who takes the initiative—God it is who seeks man. Trying to express somehow this inexpressible intimacy, the sacred text tells us that Everlasting speaks to Moses "face to face." But let us be careful: this does not mean that Moses sees the face of God. Here below, none can see the face of God and live (Ex 33:20). This belief is basic to the Old as well as the New Testament. The direct vision of God's face is reserved for the world to come: "We walk by faith and not by sight" (2 Cor 5:7); "We see now through a mirror in an obscure manner, but then face to face. Now I know in part, but then I shall know even as I am known" (1 Cor 13:12). The plenitude of happiness is reserved for what we call heaven. This is what we hear from St. Peter, too: "Him, though you have not seen, you love. In him, though you do not see him, yet believing, you exult with an unspeakable joy" (1 Pt 1:8). And St. Irenaeus writes: "For our face will see the face of the living God and will rejoice with an unspeakable joy. It will behold what constitutes its happiness" (*Adv. Haer.* V, 7, 2).

Moses, then, is "face to face" with God, that is, in God's presence—a presence quite unique, more intimate than that experienced by any other prophet.

When Miriam and Aaron, Moses' sister and brother, challenge this privilege of their brother's, the Books of Numbers relates God's words:

If there be among you a prophet, I will appear to him in a vision or I will speak to him in a dream. But it is not so with my servant Moses, who is most faithful in all my house.

For I speak to him mouth to mouth, and plainly, and not by riddles and figures doth he see the glory of Everlasting. [Nm 12:6–8][3]

The passage we quoted before has an expression more explicit still: God speaks to Moses "as a man is wont to speak to his

[3] In Dt 18:9, 15, we read a promise made by Moses: "When you are come to the land which Everlasting, your God, will give you . . . Everlasting, your God, will raise up a prophet like me: him you will hear." The Jews remember this promise in the days of Christ: "Are you the prophet?" the delegation sent from Jerusalem inquires of John the Baptist. After the multiplication of the loaves, the crowd exclaims, in reference to Jesus, "This is indeed the prophet that is to come into the world" (Jn 6:14). And when in Jerusalem they argue about Jesus, some say, "This is truly the prophet," while others reply, "Can a prophet come from Galilee?" (Jn 7:40, 42). In the Acts, finally, first Peter and then Stephen quote this passage from Deuteronomy to testify about Jesus (Acts 3:22–23, and 7:37).

friend." This divine friendship will one day be extended through Jesus' mediation to the apostles: "I have called you friends because all things that I have heard from my Father I have made known to you" (Jn 15:15).

Friendship, then, is what characterizes Moses' interviews with Everlasting when he is within the mysterious Meeting Tent.

To us, this Tent conjures up the intimacy of prayer in which all of us, God's children, appear before our Father's face and hold friendly intercourse with him.

THE SECOND FORTY-DAY PERIOD

At this point we are introduced to Moses' second forty-day retreat. He is requested by God to hew two stone slabs similar to those he has broken and to meet God again on the mountain. "Be ready . . . [to] stand with me upon the top of the mountain," says Exodus (34:2). The first period involved a divine revelation, and the climate was appropriate to a meeting between a creature and the ineffable manifestation of God. This second period would rather suggest a time of atonement and intercession. And yet, it is precisely this second period that brings about one of the most beautiful theophanies of the whole Old Testament; for penitence often results in the most exquisite outpourings of divine love.

After several petitions in the Meeting Tent following those we have already mentioned and which have seemed to us a sort of contest with God, Moses makes a request which is very touching and at the same time full of yearning: "Lord, show me your glory!"

God's glory? Glory, we would say, is the divine attribute that can be apprehended by man. But how can Moses dare make such a request? It must be the intimacy of his retreat on Mount Sinai

36

that gives him the courage and makes him thus yearn for God. He is asking for something undoubtedly more important and perhaps more concrete than he has obtained in the Meeting Tent. This man hungers for God and would know him as well as he can be known here below.

And God said: "I will make all my beauty pass before you, and in your presence I will pronounce my name: Everlasting; I who show favor to whom I will, I who grant mercy to whom I will. . . .

"But my face you cannot see, for no man sees me and still lives.

"Here," continued Everlasting, "is a place near me where you will station yourself on the rock. When my glory passes, I will set you in the hollow of the rock and will cover you with my hand until I have passed by. Then I will remove my hand so that you may see my back. But my face is not to be seen."[4] [Ex 33:19–23]

This passage is certainly very old. It conveys to us in human terms very important biblical realities. The name that God pronounces as he passes by stands for his Person.

God comes in the supreme freedom of his sovereign grace, and man must accept the initiative of his love: "I who show favor to whom I will, I who grant mercy to whom I will." He comes near man, but remains God. And this is precisely why his nearness is so precious. The vision of his face is reserved for the life that is to come: no one can see it here below and survive the experience. This is exactly true. Even in the Gospel the Father cannot be seen. It is his word that can be heard—at the Baptism of Christ, for instance, or at the Transfiguration on the mountain (which is the Sinai of the New Testament). Moses, hidden in the hollow of the rock, his eyes covered by God's hands (that is, protected by God), will behold some measure of this divine glory that vivifies man.

---

[4] This passage [in French] differs somewhat from Father Couroyer's translation of the Bible of Jerusalem. The same is to be said of Ex 34:5–7 and 29–35 later in this chapter.

And then in what depths of adoration will Moses be plunged, in what an indescribable joy!

Having come down in a cloud, Everlasting stood with him there and proclaimed his name: "Everlasting!" Thus Everlasting passed before him, and he cried out: "Everlasting! Everlasting! a merciful and gracious God, slow to anger and rich in kindness and fidelity, continuing his kindness for a thousand generations and forgiving wickedness and crime and sin; yet not declaring the guilty guiltless but punishing children and grandchildren to the third and fourth generation for their fathers' wickedness!" [Ex 34:5-7]

God chastises only the impenitent. In the largeness of his love (four generations for the punishment, but thousands of generations for the grace) he is slow to anger and infinite in mercy and truth. The light of this revelation emanating from God will henceforth mark the whole religion of Israel. It will enlighten the prophets and transform itself into prayer in the Psalms. Its beams will still fall even on the Gospels. In truth, God is really known only in his love. When at the end of this long tradition, with the knowledge the Israelites have gained of God's love and fidelity, St. John introduces Jesus in the Prologue to his Gospel, he says:

[The Word] was the true light that enlightens every man. . . .

And the Word was made flesh, and pitched his tent among us,[5] and we saw his glory—glory received from the Father as his only-begotten Son—full of grace and truth. . . .

And of his fullness we have all received, grace upon grace; for the law was given through Moses; grace and truth came through Jesus Christ. No one has at any time seen God: the only-begotten Son, who is in the bosom of the Father, he has revealed him to us. [Jn 1:9, 14, 16-18]

Here, then, does God's revelation to Moses on Mount Sinai have its fulfillment. God led his People across the desert from

[5] Literal translation.

38

within what was characteristically called the Meeting Tent. But here, in St. John's Gospel, God goes farther: the Word, the Light of God, has pitched his tent in our midst, and we have seen his "glory." This glory is the glory of the Son, and its rays emanate from the Father. Such is God's faithful and persevering love; such is God's gratuitous and merciful grace, bestowed upon us as the fulfillment of his long-pursued designs, bestowed upon us when he gave us his only-begotten Son.

Moses promulgated the Law, and the Law was intended as training, a path leading in the direction of grace. No man has seen the Father; no, not even in the Gospels, as we were saying. But the Son, "the brightness of his glory and the image of his substance" (Heb. 1:3), we have seen. "We have beheld him, touched him with our own hands, sat at table with him" (1 Jn 1:1). At the Last Supper he says, "Philip, he who sees me sees also the Father" (Jn 14:9).

What does Moses do on the mountain as God approaches him in such astonishing manner? He prostrates himself, his face in the dust. Surely he is all lost in God, you would imagine. But listen to his whispered request:

If really I have found favor with you, O Lord, do come along in our company.

This is indeed a stiff-necked people; yet pardon our wickedness and sin, and make us your own inheritance! [Ex 34:9]

You see? Moses is a shepherd and can never forget his flock— even in the midst of his most divine and personal experiences. He acknowledges the lapse but sues for mercy. What a touching phrase, "make us your own inheritance," and how well he now knows the secret of God's heart!

This great chapter of Exodus ends with these words: "Moses stayed there with Everlasting forty days and forty nights, without eating or drinking; and he wrote on the tablets the words of the Covenant" (Ex 34:28). Fasting and prayer, then, prepare for God's grace; the word of God is a refreshment; and his presence fills everything with light and life.

The Veiled Face

It is easy to understand how this sojourn on the mountain has left a mark on Moses: he has become God's own confidant. We watch him now return to the plain, his face beaming, his heart strengthened for his task. He is a changed man. As for the People, they are awe-struck and keep their distance. It is a fact that in this life mysteries cannot shine in all their brilliance. Every manifestation of God begins by troubling us.

Moses, let us point out, carries with him at the end of this second forty-day retreat the tablets of the testimony.

As Moses came down from the mountain with the tablets of the testimony in his hands, he did not know that the skin of his face had become radiant while he conversed with Everlasting.

When Aaron, then, and the other Israelites saw Moses and noticed how radiant the skin of his face had become, they were afraid to come near him.

Only after Moses called to them did Aaron and all the rulers of the community come back to him. Moses then spoke to them.

Later on all the Israelites came up to him, and he enjoined on them all that Everlasting had told him on Mount Sinai.

When he finished speaking with them, he put a veil over his face.

Whenever Moses entered the presence of Everlasting to converse with him, he removed the veil until he came out again. On coming out he would tell the Israelites all that had been commanded. Then the Israelites would see that the skin of Moses' face was radiant, so he would again put the veil over his face until he went in to converse with Everlasting. [Ex 34:29–35]

The mediator's face is veiled, then, but the veil is removed when prayer renews contact with God—veiled before men, unveiled during intercourse with Everlasting. The Bible simply says this extraordinary thing: to speak with God. And Moses repeats faithfully to his people all that Everlasting has commanded.

Solitude and prayer, glory and grace—divine words. Such are the elements that make up Moses' second quarantine.

THE LORD OF GLORY

One day, following in Moses' footsteps, I climbed to the top of Djebel Mousa. A gorgeous vista opened out before me. After reading once more the sacred account of God's revelation to Moses, I proceeded to the summit of the rock, toward the little chapel built there by the Orthodox monks of the Sinai Monastery. I dressed the altar in the narrow entrance porch; I brought on the bread and wine. The holy sacrifice began. After the readings and the prayers, the priest bowed over the altar: "This is my body," I whispered; "This is my blood."

Jesus, the Lord of glory, descended then in our midst, in the mystery of the New and Eternal Covenant, and *"nos plebs tua sancta"* received holy communion. Then, "With faces unveiled, reflecting as in a mirror the glory of the Lord, we are transformed into his very image, from glory to glory (2 Cor 3:18).

These are the mysteries with which our own Lenten retreats ought to harmonize more and more as we proceed on our earthly journey.

THE PEOPLE OF THE COVENANT

In the prophetic meditation of Deuteronomy, we read these words addressed by Moses to his People:

Be earnestly on your guard not to forget the things which your own eyes have seen, nor let them slip from your memory as long as you live, but teach them to your children and to your children's children.

There was the day when you stood before Everlasting, your God, at Horeb, and he said to me: "Assemble the people for me: I will have them hear my words that they may learn to fear me as long as they live in the land and may so teach their children."

And you came to the foot of the mountain, which blazed to the very sky with fire and was enveloped in a dense black cloud.

Then Everlasting spoke to you from the midst of the fire. You heard the sound of the words but saw no form. There was only a voice. And [Everlasting] proclaimed to you his Covenant, which he commanded you to keep: the Ten Commandments, which he wrote on two tablets of stone.

Everlasting charged me at that time to teach you the statutes and decrees which you are to observe over in the land you will occupy. [Dt 4:9–14]

This passage recounts the great basic events forming the Covenant.

And the following words, the holiest for the People of Israel, contain the great prayer that has resounded within all faithful hearts, the prayer that has been whispered or proclaimed on all important occasions in the religion and the life of God's People:

Hear, O Israel: Everlasting is our God, Everlasting alone.

Therefore you will love Everlasting, your God, with all your heart and with all your soul and with all your strength.

Take to heart these words which I enjoin on you today.

Repeat them to your children. Speak of them at home and abroad, whether you are busy or at rest. Bind them at your wrist as a sign, and let them be as a pendant on your forehead. Write them on the doorpost of your houses and on your gates. [Dt 6:4–7]

The Jewish people have given this commandment a literal interpretation. This prayer is to be found written on the inner door of the closet in which the Torah[6] is kept in their synagogues (thus becoming, as it were, an exergue of the holy Scriptures). When at prayer, faithful Jews wear the words of this prayer on their foreheads and wrists in leather bands. No one should smile at this. Nothing acts automatically in religion, of course, but a people who allow themselves to be spiritually influenced to this degree by the love of God would truly be the People of God:

For you are a people sacred to Everlasting, your God. He has chosen you from all the nations on the face of the earth to be a people peculiarly his own.

It was not because you are the largest of all nations that Everlasting has set his heart on you and chosen you . . . . It was because Everlasting loved you . . . . [Dt 7:6–8]

[6] The Torah or Pentateuch is the five books of Moses, that is, the first five books of the Old Testament.

Elias' Journey

[Elias] walked . . . forty days and forty nights unto the mount of God, Horeb. [3 K 19:8]

Soon after the death of Solomon, the unity of the kingdom of the People of Israel began to collapse—and, in fact, would never be completely restored. The nation divided itself: the ten tribes in the north formed themselves into the kingdom of Israel, and and the two tribes in the south, around Jerusalem, became the kingdom of Judah.

God saw to it, however, that prophets appeared in both kingdoms where kings, in Judah especially, kept the desire for reunion alive.

After a most difficult period of some fifty years, about 880 B.C. the two tiny nations experienced a time of material prosperity.

In the north, Omri, king of Israel, built a capital city, Samaria, intended as a rival to Jerusalem. Nestling on a beautiful hill a few miles from Sichem and Jacob's well, the city became rather important, and the Royal Palace had real grandeur. Omri's son was the famed King Achab who married Jezabel, the daughter of the king of Tyre and Sidon. This princess, a pagan, had her own gods and priests, and established the worship of Baal within the precincts of the Royal Palace itself.

It is in this region at this time and under King Achab that Elias, the prophet, exercised his prophetic ministry.[1] A prophet is a man who speaks of God, reminds men of God, converts souls

[1] See *Élie le Prophète, selon les Écritures et les Traditions chrétiennes* (Desclée de Brouwer); Roger Breuil, *La Puissance d'Élie* (Delachaux et Niestlé); and Roger Poelman, *Élie le Prophète* (Elsevier).

to Everlasting. A prophet wields power: he works miracles, forms or reforms a people's faith, guides its hope, and points out to it the way of true love.

THE SACRIFICE ON MOUNT CARMEL

When Elias the Thesbite makes his appearance, the true religion itself is at stake. God is one; religion is one. Earlier, Solomon allowed Temples to be built in Jerusalem to the gods of his concubines. Today one can still observe on the slopes of Mount Olivet the "Hill of Scandal," the site of this idol worship, so shocked was Israel's conscience. But now Achab goes farther still: he shares in his wife's idolatry and "goes himself after the baals."[2] Not that he completely rejects Everlasting—him *too* he worships. With this compromise, everything seems to be lost, for God has not interfered. Israel is no longer a People set apart. They no longer have a divine vocation, and the Covenant is a thing of the past. Where is the love, the jealous love of God? "How long will you limp with both legs? If Everlasting is God, follow him; if it is Baal, follow him" (3 K 18:21).

Elias will be the principal prophet of the Covenant. He will campaign vehemently for a return to the religion of Sinai. The Books of Kings relate these activities of the prophet soon after they have taken place. The descriptions of his rigorous actions still pulsate with the breath of life.

The instant he appears, Elias shows that he is endowed with a power reminding us of Moses'. At his command there is a drought, parched land, and famine. It seems as if the plagues of Egypt were beginning anew. The Bible describes with dramatic force the frightful judgment enacted on Mount Carmel.

[2] Baal is the god of Canaan and the patron of the city of Tyre. In Palestine there were several temples built to him. Hence the plural *baals*.

Elias has summoned to the summit of the mountain all the people and all the priests of Baal. He is Everlasting's only man among the idol's four hundred and fifty priests. Let them build an altar, he challenges; let them sacrifice a victim; let them call upon their Baal and see if he will hear them and send a flame to consume the victim!

In the biblical narrative the issue at stake is of supreme importance. Even for us who read it, in a way, the identity of the true God is in question.

Achab sent to all the children of Israel, and gathered together the prophets unto Mount Carmel.

And Elias coming to all the people said: "How long will you limp with both legs? If Everlasting is God, follow him; if it is Baal, follow him." And the people did not answer him a word. [3 K 18:20-21]

And now the prophet throws out his defiant challenge. A dramatic silence follows. Everyone understands clearly what the question implies. No man can serve two masters.

And Elias said again to the people: "Only I remain a prophet of Everlasting, but the prophets of Baal are four hundred and fifty men. Let two bullocks be given us and let them choose one bullock for themselves, and cut it in pieces and put it upon wood, but put no fire under; and I will dress the other bullock and lay it upon wood and put no fire under it. Call on the names of your gods and I will call on the name of Everlasting, and the God that will answer by fire, let him be God."

And all the people, answering, said: "A very good proposal."

Then Elias said to the prophets of Baal: "Choose you first, because you are many." [3 K 18:22-25]

We now witness the pagan scene. Baal's priests prepare their victim and commence their prayers and incantations. Elias whips them with his taunts while in the frenzy of their mystic rites they slash their flesh to earn the idol's good will. But the result is silence and emptiness.

And they took the bullock and dressed it, and they called on the name of Baal from morning even till noon, saying: O Baal, hear us! But there was no voice nor any that answered: and they leaped over the altar that they had made.

And when it was now noon, Elias jested at them, saying: "Cry with a louder voice, for he is a god, and perhaps is talking or busy, or on a journey, or perhaps he is asleep and must be awakened."

So they cried with a loud voice and cut themselves after their manner with knives and lancets, till they were covered all with blood.

And after midday was past, and while they were prophesying, the time was come of offering sacrifice, and there was no voice heard, nor did anyone answer nor regard them as they prayed. [3 K 18:26–29]

The time of offering sacrifice corresponds to the evening sacrifice as prescribed by ritual: "Two unblemished yearling lambs each day as the established holocaust, offering one lamb in the morning and the other during the evening twilight" (Nm 18:4). At this hour, after all the useless excitement of the day, Elias comes forth, and all eyes are upon him. He is the prophet of the true God, come to restore the Covenant, and he begins by erecting an altar according to the code of the Covenant:

And he took twelve stones according to the number of the tribes of the sons of Jacob to whom the word of God came, saying: "Israel will be thy name;" and he built an altar to the name of Everlasting. [3 K 18:31–32]

In all these details we can see the faithfulness of the man. It is noteworthy that in spite of the People's division into two kingdoms, the religion of the true God still regards the twelve tribes as united: twelve stones are assembled into a single altar. Water is now poured on the altar, on the wood, and on the victim. With this Elias intends to display the intervention of God more forcefully. There follows the prayer of the prophet. The people hear him call upon the one God, him who in the past has intervened in human affairs, and demand his answer so that all may believe in him. The People have fallen into sinful ways; it is God alone who can convert their hearts.

And when it was time to offer the holocaust, Elias the prophet came near and said:

"O Everlasting, God of Abraham and Isaac and Israel, show this day that you are the God of Israel and I your servant, and that according to your commandment I have done all these things.

"Hear me, Everlasting, hear me: that these people may learn that you, Everlasting, are God, and that you have turned their heart again." [3 K 18:36–37]

Fire descends from heaven in a devouring flame, and in a minute everything is over. The people make again their choice. The God of the Covenant has manifested his power as he did on Sinai "in a flame of fire out of the midst of a bush" (Ex 3:2), or again on the mountain in the great desert manifestation: "All Mount Sinai was in smoke because Everlasting was come upon it in fire, and the smoke arose from it as out of a furnace, and all the mountain shook violently" (Ex 19:18). Surely it is Everlasting, the God of the fathers, who has chosen the People. He it is who has once more revealed Himself. The Covenant, then, is valid still![3]

[3] Jesus will say, "I have come to cast fire upon earth, and what will I but that it be kindled?" (Lk 12:49); and on Pentecost, the Spirit will descend on the apostles in the shape of tongues of fire (Acts 2:3).

TAEDIUM VITAE

The slaughter of all Baal's priests that follows reminds us of the death of the firstborn of Egypt on the first Passover. Finally, an abundant rain falls at the request of God's servant and restores life to the land and the people.

One person, however, is not at all satisfied with the turn of events—Jezabel. She it is who brings about Elias' forty-day retreat.

And Achab told Jezabel all that Elias had done, and how he had slain all the prophets with the sword. Then Jezabel sent a messenger to Elias, saying: "Such and such things may the gods do to me, and add still more, if by this hour tomorrow I make not your life as the life of one of them."

Then Elias was afraid, and rising up he went away to save his life. And he came to Bersabee of Judah and left his servant there, and he went forward one day's journey into the desert. And when he was there and sat under a juniper tree, he requested for his soul that he might die, and said:

"It is enough for me, Everlasting! Take away my life, for I am no better than my fathers." And he cast himself down and slept. [3 K 19:1-4]

Elias has to flee as Moses had to flee. Like the great mediator of the first Covenant of Sinai, so Elias now is a prey to utter discouragement; as Moses one day wished to die, so does Elias now. Even Jesus, one day, will be sad unto death (Mt 26:37-38). This is the frightful *taedium vitae*—the weariness of life, the I-can't-any-more that we all may experience at times. There seems to be no more hope, nothing more worth living for; the sleep of death seems a thing to prefer. And yet, this moment of despair may be a moment of God's grace.

49

THE BREAD FOR THE ROAD

And behold, an angel touched him and said to him: "Arise and eat."

He looked, and behold there was at his head a hearth cake and a vessel of water; and he ate and drank and he fell asleep again.

And the angel of Everlasting came again a second time and touched him and said to him: "Arise, eat, for you have a great way to go."

And he arose and ate and drank, and walked in the strength of that food forty days and forty nights unto the mount of God, Horeb. [1 K 19:5–8]

At the moment of Christ's supreme discouragement, God will also send an angel to him in the Garden of Olives. Scripture introduces the angel here in the act of rousing Elias asleep in the desert. And he arises and eats and drinks to be able to walk to the mountain of God. What kind of bread is this, and what kind of water? Manna that descends again in the desert? Water that flows again from the rock? May Elias eat his bread, and may he learn, as his people have for forty years, man's utter dependence on God. "You have a great way to go. . . ." What way? The way that leads to the mountain of revelation—Horeb, or Sinai, the place where God appears to his elect.

In any case, this bread is bread for the road. It takes forty days and forty nights to cover the distance to the Lord.

Elias at last reaches the mountain of Moses. There he is climbing, alone, an ant among the enormous boulders of reddish rock. Watch him now as he enters a hollow, almost lost among the towering crags. A cave yawns in the side of the rocky wall. That is where the prophet spends the night. One is reminded of Moses in the hollow of the rock before his great personal religious experience. One is also reminded of Christ: "He went up the mountain by himself to pray. And when it was late, he was there alone" (Mt 14:23).

RENEWED VOCATION

Elias has not journeyed in vain. He has come to God's meeting place, and Everlasting's voice now falls upon his ears:

"What are you doing here, Elias?"

And he answered: "With zeal have I been zealous for Everlasting, God of hosts; for the children of Israel have forsaken your Covenant; they have thrown down your altars, they have slain your prophets with the sword, and I am left, and they seek my life to take it away."

And he said to him: "Go forth and stand upon the mountain before Everlasting." [3 K 19:9–10]

What is Elias doing on the mountain at the end of his journey? He has come—as a last remnant, he says—to find shelter at the site of the Covenant. "Go forth and stand . . . before Everlasting." Come, now, since he has called you, and stand in the presence of God.

And behold, Everlasting passed.

And there came a strong wind before Everlasting, overthrowing the mountains and breaking the rocks to pieces, and Everlasting was not in the wind.

And after the wind an earthquake, but Everlasting was not in the earthquake.

And after the earthquake a fire, but Everlasting was not in the fire.

And after the fire a whistling of a gentle air.

And when Elias heard it he covered his face with his mantle, and coming forth, stood in the entrance of the cave. And behold, a voice came unto him, saying: . . . .

"Go, and return on your way through the desert to Damascus. And when you are come thither, you shall anoint Hazael to be king over Aram. And you shall anoint Jehu, the son of Namsi, to be king over Israel; and Eliseus, the son of Saphat of Abel Mehola, you shall anoint to be prophet in your place." [3 K 19:11–13, 15–16]

How should we interpret so mysterious a passage?

To begin with, God appears to Elias. Thus he has appeared in Eden "at the afternoon air" (Gn 3:8) to talk with Adam; he has come to Noah before the Deluge and the fresh start after the flood, to Abraham for a blessing unto all nations, and to Moses for the liberation of Israel and the Covenant with his People. He will come in the person of Jesus, his only-begotten Son, for the salvation of the world; and this Son will come in his glory for a final rendezvous with mankind. Thus God comes now to Elias among the rock of Horeb-Sinai.

How does he come? In quite a different way from what we would expect. There are warning signs—the storm, the earthquake, the fire. Jesus will also mention cosmic upheavals as introducing his parousia (Mt 24:29–30). These signs are intended to keep us watchful. But it is not in them that the coming itself consists. Let us rest assured: when it is he who comes, there will be no mistaking him. The last warning sign to Elias is the sigh of a gentle breeze, almost like the "afternoon air" of Eden when God came to chat with man. The prophet now leaves his cave and covers his face, just as Moses did before the burning bush.

Elias is now in the intimacy of God's presence, a divine manifestation, completely interior, completely immaterial: the voice that is heard is the voice of God. And the voice unfolds a whole program of work. Elias, who wished to die, who had "had enough," is sent back to the People to carry out the great actions of God's diplomacy. He must depose two kings, one of them a foreigner, and anoint new men of God's choosing. He must also seek out Eliseus and anoint him as his helper with right of succession in the prophetic ministry.

Go forth, then, Elias! God sends up and gives you his strength for the task. You have resumed contact with the great realities of the Covenant. Go forth! March on! Through you the designs of a loving God will be carried out.

This idea of a route and a journey, consequent upon the manifestation of God, dominates Elias' awesome forty-day retreat. He is Moses' associate in the divine revelation of Horeb-Sinai. Both of them will appear again with Christ as witnesses in the New Testament on the Mountain of the Transfiguration. On that occasion, the three favored apostles will hear again the voice of the Father, experience something of the glory of the Son, and be made partakers of the secrets of love.

THE TRANSFIGURATION

Let us first of all examine the significance of the account of the Transfiguration and the place it holds in the chain of events is St. Matthew's Gospel.

Christ's public life begins with the announcement of the Beatitudes, or with the whole Sermon on the Mount. The Kingdom of God is about to begin, and this is its charter. Then comes the "day of the Parables:" the thirteenth chapter of St. Matthew contains seven parables on the mystery of the Kingdom and its advent. This is an unexpected turn of events, and people are deeply disappointed; they have been looking forward to a kingdom of glory, and here is Christ treating them to stories so childish and apparently so trite—a woman kneading her bread, a fisherman casting his nets, a peasant sowing his seed. What should they make of all this? The crowd deserts him.

As for the apostles themselves, they ask, "Explain to us these parables." And that is precisely what Christ wants. The parable is an introduction to a deeper, more detailed explanation. And to them, who are really interested in the Kingdom, he reveals the king as well. From the fourteenth to the sixteenth chapter Christ draws all the light upon himself. He works unheard of miracles: twice multiplies loaves, walks on the lake, heals the daughter of the Canaanite woman. Finally he inquires, "Who do men say the Son of man is?" (Mt 16:13). He has in fact a more important truth to reveal and dares not, will not reveal it until he is sure they have recognized him for what he is; for only then will they believe what he has to tell them.

Christ's question draws Peter's great answer: "You are the Christ, the Son of the living God" (Mt 16:16). At this moment Peter has allowed himself to be enlightened by the Father in heaven, and with his new faith he can now receive the message: "From that time Jesus began to show that he must go to Jerusalem and suffer many things from the elders and scribes and chief priests, and be put to death, and on the third day rise again" (Mt 16:21–23).

Here we are, now, face to face with the real mystery of Christ's mission. It is staggering. He is going to celebrate a new Pasch, cement a New Covenant between God and man with his own blood. "And Peter, taking him aside, began to chide him saying: 'Far be it from you, O Lord; this will never happen to you.' " And Christ, who has just praised him because he has let himself be enlightened by the Father, reproaches him now: "You do not mind the things of God but those of men."

Peter's shock is understandable. If this is going to be the fate of the Master, what will be in store for his faithful disciples? "Then Jesus said to his disciples: 'If anyone wishes to come after me, let him deny himself and take up his cross and follow me' " (Mt 16:24).

In the logical sequence of the Gospel, the narrative of the Transfiguration finds its place here. It is linked with what has taken place before—"six days afterwards," says the Gospel, six days after the foretelling of the Passion and the Resurrection. The text of St. Matthew reads:

Now six days afterwards Jesus took Peter, James, and John and led them up a high mountain by themselves, and was transfigured before them. And his face shone as the sun, and his garment became white as snow.

And behold, there appeared to them Moses and Elias talking together with him.

Then Peter addressed Jesus, saying: "Lord, it is good for us to be here. If you will it, let us set up three tents here, one for you, one for Moses, and one for Elias."

As he was still speaking, behold, a white cloud overshadowed them, and behold, a voice out of the cloud said: "This is my beloved Son, in whom I am well pleased: hear him."

And on hearing it the disciples fell on their faces and were exceedingly afraid.

And Jesus came near and touched them, and said to them: "Arise, and do not be afraid."

But lifting up their eyes, they saw no one but Jesus only. [Mt. 17:1–8]

We immediately sense that this is a message of exceptional importance. Let us study the text more closely.

First, Christ chooses three witnesses. One of them is Peter, the brother of Andrew, who, however, is left out. Then there are the two "sons of the thunder," as Jesus has named them— James and John. These three are chosen to witness the great manifestation on the Mountain. But these same apostles will also witness Christ's supreme humiliation in the garden when, prone on the ground in utter exhaustion and a sweat of blood, he will go through his agony. Both visions are concerned with the same Lord, each as astounding as the other. Both are testimonies to the Pasch of Jesus.

The three apostles are led apart—deliberately, intentionally—up a mountain. Traditionally we associate the Transfiguration with Mount Thabor. Whatever the site, it is obvious that we have here what may be called the Sinai of the New Testament—the mountain of God's theophanies, the scene of the manifestations of God's glory. Mount Thabor is actually quite a solitary mountain. It overlooks a vast plain and dominates the whole biblical country of Galilee.

Jesus is transfigured, and his Transfiguration is truly an apocalyptic event. The angel who rolls away the stone of the sepulcher on Easter morning, will also have "his countenance like lightning and his raiment like snow" (Mt 28:3). With this event, the humanity of Christ introduces us to his glory. What was God's real purpose when he created man after his image and likeness (Gn 1:26)? For obviously all this extraordinary sequence of divine actions, and the Incarnation itself, were intended for man's benefit. The Transfiguration reveals something of the mystery that is man:

[Christ] is the image of the invisible God, the firstborn of every creature. For in him were created all things, in the heavens and on the earth, things visible and things invisible . . . . All things have been created through and unto him. [Col 1:15–16]

This manifestation of God's image is limited to the range of our finite intelligence, to be sure. By the aid of such images we are initiated into the mysteries of our faith: "For you have died and your life is hidden with Christ in God. When Christ, your life, shall appear, then you too will appear with him in glory" (Col 3:3–4).

The Transfiguration concerns us very specifically, therefore. It indicates that we know only the embryo of man, that everything here below is in a continuous Passover toward a new world, a world which we cannot imagine but which is entirely dominated by the Lord Jesus.

And here Moses and Elias, the two great authorities of the Old Testament, the two men of Sinai, come to converse with Jesus— Moses, the type of all that goes under the name of the Law, and Elias, the prototype of the prophets. How powerful and reassuring this vision is! It confirms all the theology of the Bible. Christ can only be understood against the background of the Old Testament. A single history moves to its fulfillment in the New Testament. And what do Moses and Elias speak about? St. Luke tells us: ". . . appearing in glory, [they] spoke of his exodus [his passover, his death], which he was about to fulfill in Jerusalem" (Lk 9:30).

Here, then, is the connection with the "six days afterwards," that is, after the foretelling of his Passion. Christ's glory and suffering, his death and Resurrection make up one single mystery. This double aspect reveals both God's eternal life and his association with men, with us. This double aspect is the object of Christ's discussion with Moses and Elias.

A shining cloud appears now as all during the time of God's People in the desert a pillar of light indicated the active presence and protection of Everlasting. This same cloud now veils the scene of the Transfiguration and from out of it thunders the voice of the Father. The Father introduced his only-begotten and beloved Son to us at the Jordan at the beginning of Jesus' public life; he now reveals his love again: "My beloved Son." And he also bids us listen to Christ and the message of his Gospel.

To the apostles, the vision has been a heavenly experience. Peter is already thinking of the "eternal tent," the "aeterna taber-

nacula," where God welcomes the elect.[4] But the joy is not to last. Moses' vision in the hollow of the rock did not last, either; God only passed by. St. Luke remarks that the Transfiguration has taken place "as Jesus was praying" (Lk 9:29), and adds this revealing detail: "Peter and his companions were heavy with sleep" (Lk 9:32). They will again be heavy with sleep in the Garden of Olives. In truth, we are not quite prepared as yet to "bear" the mysteries of God. It is fortunate for us that his love and patience are infinite!

And suddenly everything returns to normal, and Jesus is left alone—Jesus with his loving reassurance and his comforting nearness. Still, the mystery of his manifestation must not be forgotten:

And as they were coming down from the mountain, he cautioned them to tell no one what they had seen, except when the Son of man should have risen from the dead.

And they kept what he said to themselves, discussing with one another what the words "when he shall have risen from the dead" might mean. [Mk 9:8–9]

They cannot understand. But they remember. The Blessed Virgin, too, "remembered in her heart" the things of Christ's infancy (Lk 2:19, 51).

These are the vistas and destination to which Elias' route leads us—farther and in other paths than we would have supposed.

The Church, contemplating this mystery of her Lord on the Feast of the Transfiguration, draws freely from her Psalms and celebrates with a sense of triumph the truth she now understands in the light of the Holy Spirit:

---

[4] Harald Riesenfeld, in his *Jesus Transfigured* (Upsala, 1947), underlines the connection between this passage of the Gospel and the ritual celebration at Jerusalem of the Feast of the Tabernacles.

What is man that you are mindful of him; or the son of man that you visited him?

You have made him little less than the angels; you have crowned him with glory and honor, and have set him over the works of your hand. . . .

Everlasting, our Lord, how admirable is your name in all the earth! [Ps 8:5–7, 10]

In the nuptial Psalm (45) the Church describes her beloved. "The shining light," "the glorious one," she exclaims elsewhere in reference to Christ (Ps 76:5).

The heavens are grateful for your wonders, Everlasting. . . . For who in the clouds can be compared to Everlasting . . . ?

Yours are the heavens, and yours is the earth. . . . Thabor and Hermon will rejoice in your name.

Mercy and truth will go before your face.
Blessed is the people that knows jubilation . . . they will walk, O Everlasting, in the light of your face. . . . [Ps 89:6–7, 12–16]

Everlasting, my God, you are exceedingly great! . . . You . . . [are] clothed with light as with a garment! [Ps 104:1–2]

The Book of Jonas

Forty days more, and Nineveh will be destroyed. [Jon 3:4]

THE brief Book of Jonas (barely four chapters) brings us again to the subject of a penitential and saving forty-day period.

The forty days of the Deluge belong to the literary genre peculiar to the first eleven chapters of Genesis. Moses' retreats pertain to the period of Exodus, and are narrated in the books that go under the name of the law, while Elias' quarantine takes place during the first prophetic period in the ninth century B.C.

The little Book of Jonas is a *midrash,* a sort of parable, written probably about the time of the Jews' return from their exile, toward the end of the fifth century B.C. The populous city referred to is an allegorical Nineveh. History does not record this alleged mass conversion which, if it had really taken place, would constitute "a miracle without comparison in the annals of human history, a greater miracle than that of Pentecost" (Feuillet).

As for the author of the book, there is indeed a prophet by the name of Jonas, but nothing more is known about him than that he lived in the northern kingdom some three hundred years before the composition of the book that bears his name, during Jeroboam II's reign (4 K 14:25).

These facts, however, in no way diminish the spiritual significance of this short work, for it contains an important message. If after the Jews' return from exile we observe a strictly nationalistic trend in the work of Esdras and Nehemias ("nationalistic" in the sense given the word in *sacred* history), we also find broad missionary vistas envisioned in the writing of Jonas. The

Jews taken into captivity were astonished by their first sight of large cities, teeming with men engaged in idol worship. For the first time they found themselves faced with the problem of universalism, a corollary to faith in the oneness of God. The Second Isaias traced a path in this new direction during the years of the Exile.

When we study the literary genre of the Book of Jonas, we understand all the better the symbolic value of the number forty. A religious meaning was already attached to it: it stood for a sign of God. Let us see how this develops.

JONAS' REBELLION AGAINST HIS VOCATION

Now the word of Everlasting came to Jonas, the son of Amittai, saying: "Arise and go to Nineveh, the great city, and preach in it, for the wickedness thereof is come up before me."

And Jonas rose up to flee into Tharsis from the face of Everlasting. And he went down to Joppe and found a ship going to Tharsis, and he paid the fare thereof and went down into it to go with them to Tharsis away from Everlasting.

But Everlasting sent a great wind into the sea, and a great tempest was raised in the sea and the ship was in danger of being broken. And the mariners were afraid, and the men cried to their god; and they cast forth the wares that were in the ship, into the sea, to lighten it of them.

And Jonas went down into the inner part of the ship and fell into a deep sleep. And the shipmaster came to him and said to him: "Why are you fast asleep? Rise up, call upon your God, if it so be that God will think of us, that we may not perish."

And they said, every one to his fellow: "Come, and let us cast lots that we may know why this evil is upon us." And they cast lots and the lot fell upon Jonas. And they said to him: "Tell us for what cause this evil is upon us. What is your business? Of what country are you? And where are you going? Or of what people are you?"

And he said to them: "I am a Hebrew, and I fear Everlasting, the God of heaven, who made both the sea and the dry land."

And the men were greatly afraid, and said to him: "Why have you done this?" (For they knew that he fled from the face of Everlasting, because he had told them.) And they said to him: "What shall we do to you that the sea may be calm to us?" For the sea flowed and swelled.

And he said to them: "Take me up and cast me into the sea, and the sea will be calm to you; for I know that for my sake this great tempest is upon you."

And the men rowed hard to return to land, but they were not able, because the sea tossed and swelled upon them. And they cried to Everlasting and said: "We beseech thee, O Everlasting, let us not perish for this man's life, and lay not upon us innocent blood, for you, O Everlasting, have done as it pleased you."

And they took Jonas and cast him into the sea, and the sea ceased from raging. And the men feared Everlasting exceedingly, and sacrificed victims to Everlasting, and made vows. [Jon 1]

God chooses his prophet and plans to send him to Nineveh. Nineveh is a hostile city; it has already been the cause of great misfortune to Israel. Since God is concerned with the whole world, however, Jonas must preach penance to the Ninevites. Their sinfulness has risen to God, like the sinfulness of mankind before the Deluge.

Jonas, not in the least enthusiastic about his mission, tries to fly from it. He proceeds to Joppe, and there we watch him looking for a boat, paying his fare, and sailing away. He sails for Tharsis. Where is Tharsis? It is beyond Crete, Cyprus, or any other region he has heard about; it is a vague place; Tharsis means the unknown, the world's end, a place far from Everlasting.

One might meditate here on the words of the psalm:

O Everlasting, you have probed me and you know me. You know when I sit and when I stand; You understand my thoughts from afar.

My journeys and my rest you scrutinize; with all my ways you are familiar. . . .

Behind and before you hem me in and rest your hand upon me. . . .

Where can I go from your Spirit? . . .

If I settle at the farthest limits of the sea, even there your hand will guide me, and your right hand will hold me fast. [Ps 139:1–3, 5, 7, 9–10]

Jonas will find this out for himself.

The boatmen belong to different race and worship different gods. Note, however, that none of them is said to be without a god. That would make no sense to a Hebrew.

Jonas is unaware of what is happening; he is asleep. The storm is sent by God himself. How can they escape it? Jonas might well shirk his duty, but he is not an apostate. To the boatmen's queries he gives a precise answer: "I am a Hebrew," he says, "and I fear Everlasting, the God of heaven"—heaven for him is God's dwelling; it is there that God resides—"who made both the sea and the dry land;" in short, all created things. Hence he can control even these raging waves.

This profession of faith is beautiful concise, and universal, and can thus be understood by these pagan sailors. Fear seizes them when they hear that Jonas has thus disobeyed Everlasting, for the prophet has told them all that has happened. They endeavor in vain to save him by making for the shore, but, exhausted, they finally decide to throw him overboard. As they do so, they offer a prayer to God, for they do not know what to think and can no longer tell good from evil. Finally, they offer sacrifices and make vows.

These pagans are strangely upright and religious in comparison to Jonas, who professes the true faith and yet disobeys the command of his God.

JONAS' RESCUE

Now Everlasting prepared a great fish to swallow up Jonas. And Jonas was in the belly of the fish three days and three nights. And Jonas prayed to Everlasting, his God, out of the belly of the fish, and said:

"I cried out of my affliction to Everlasting, and he heard me; I cried out of the belly of Sheol,[1] and you have heard my voice.

"You had cast me forth into the deep in the heart of the sea, and a flood had compassed me: all your billows and your waves have passed over me.

"And I said: 'I am cast away of the sight of your eyes. How shall I see again your holy temple?'

"The waters had compassed me about even to my soul, the deep had closed me round about, and the seaweed had covered my head, at the base of the mountains.

"I had descended into subterranean lands, among the men of ancient times; and you have brought me up to life, O Everlasting, my God.

"When my soul was in distress within me, I remembered Everlasting, and my prayer has come to you, unto your holy temple. Those who serve their vanity forfeit their own grace.

"But I with the voice of praise will sacrifice to you. I will pay whatever I have vowed. From Everlasting comes salvation."

And Everlasting spoke to the fish, who vomited up Jonas upon the dry land. [Jon 2]

This psalm, probably a later addition to the Book of Jonas, is a prayer that rises from the depths, and one of the great biblical invocations of God. After the temptation to despair comes complete trust in God, even in the most terrible trial, even in the shadow of death, even on the threshold of the grave. The prayer of the unhappy soul is thus a liturgical prayer: it finds its way

[1] Sheol is the dark place of the dead.

to the temple from the very bottom of the sea. If the man of God is given life, it is only that he might participate in the sacred liturgy of the temple in supplication and thanksgiving.

This is another lesson that the People of God learned in their Exile: they discovered their priestly vocation; they are a people destined to praise God.

The theme of this prayer is clear. It is a miracle of sheer grace that God has saved his prophet. Jonas has found himself at grips with death: seaweed was choking him, the bolt was drawn . . . and after three day he was restored to life.[2]

Jesus, the Messiah, will refer to this "sign of Jonas" in his Gospel to prepare us for the mystery of his death and Resurrection:

An evil and adulterous generation demands a sign, and no sign will be given it but the sign of Jonas the prophet.

For even as Jonas was in the belly of the fish three days and three nights, so will the Son of man be three days and three nights in the heart of the earth.

The men of Nineveh will rise up in the judgment with this generation and will condemn it, for they repented at the preaching of Jonas, and behold, a greater than Jonas is here. [Mt. 12:39–41]

Jesus here applies to himself the surrender to death as well as the preaching and the resulting conversion that are described in this passage of the Bible. It would be foolish to try to ignore the supernatural character this *midrash* emphasizes. The parable is explained by Jesus who sees his own life foreshadowed in it. We need only think of the Son of God's being consigned for three days to the grave in the womb of the earth of the stone sealing

---

[2] "Jonas' fish, like Elias' crow or Balaam's ass, represents the animal world put to the service of the prophets to lend authenticity to their mission" (Feuillet).

the tomb, of the guards keeping watch, and the author of life's being plunged into death.[3]

NINEVEH'S CONVERSION AND GOD'S FORGIVENESS

After this misadventure, the prophet is ready to fulfill God's will to the letter.

And the word of Everlasting came to Jonas the second time, saying: "Arise and go to Nineveh, the great city, and preach in it the preaching that I bid you."

And Jonas arose and went to Nineveh according to the word of Everlasting. Now, Nineveh was a great city of three days' journey. And Jonas began to enter into the city one day's journey, and he cried and said: "Forty days more, and Nineveh will be destroyed."

And the men of Nineveh believed in God, and they proclaimed a fast and put on sackcloth from the greatest to the least.

And the word came to the king of Nineveh, and he rose up out of his throne and cast away his robe from him and was clothed in sackcloth and sat in ashes; and he caused it to be proclaimed and published in Nineveh from the mouth of the king and of his princes, saying:

"Let neither men nor beasts, oxen nor sheep, taste anything; let them not feed or drink water. And let men and beasts be covered with sackcloth and cry to the Lord with all their strength, and let them every one turn from their evil ways and from the iniquity that is in their hands. Who can tell if God will turn and forgive, and will turn away from his fierce anger, and we shall not perish?" [Jon 3:1–9]

All Jonas' efforts this time are bent on delivering God's message exactly. He has to proclaim a last respite of forty days.

---

[3] There is a long series of beautiful biblical passages on prayer from the grave and deliverance from the land of death: Ps 87, Joseph (Gn 42:21 and Wis 10:13–14), Jer 38:1–13, and Dn 6. See *Spiritualité pascale* (Desclée), pp. 180–189.

And here we are again with this number symbolic of penance, fasting, and prayer.

The prophet goes through the city in three days of walking. From the very first day the Ninevites believe in God, and their faith yields forth repentance. They believe in Jonas' word and thus enter into the designs of Everlasting.

Penance takes its usual course: fasting to begin with, then the replacement of garments with sackcloth. Fine raiment denotes rejoicing, sackcloth stands for penance and mourning, and the hair shirt stands for mortification. The whole city takes part in this forty-day penance, from the greatest to the humblest, beginning with the king himself.

Animals, too, must share in this human spiritual experience. The account of Noah and the Deluge has already suggested it. In the Book of Judith, we find a still more remarkable account:

And all the men of Israel cried with one accord to Everlasting, and they humbled themselves before him. They and their wives, their children and beasts and every living thing around them, mercenaries and slaves, girt their loins in sackcloth.

And all the Israelites of Jerusalem, women and children as well, prostrated themselves on the ground before the sanctuary, and covered their heads with ashes and extended their hands before Everlasting; and the altar itself they covered with haircloth.

And they cried with one accord and great earnestness to the God of Israel. [Jud 4:9–12]

These exterior gestures enable us to enter into the spirit of the occasion. It is man with all his environment of living things who stands before the Lord. The Church has inherited these ashes and scatters them on the foreheads of the faithful at the beginning of Lent, and she places a penitential garb on her priests and her altars.

Prayer consists, in the Book of Jonas as well as in that of Judith, in "crying out to God," or in "crying toward God." It is a vocal prayer, simple but sincere, full of faith, repentance, hope, and petition.

The final aspect of this forty-day period of penance emphasizes its deep spiritual significance: "They humbled their souls in fasting and prayer." This involves a complete program of spiritual regeneration; it implies recognition of guilt and the turning away from the evil path and violent deeds. Clearly, this is not a conventional or exterior pose, or merely a ritual; it is the whole soul of man, his whole spirit, that turns to God. The third chapter concludes:

And God saw their works, that they were turned from their evil ways; and God had mercy with regard to the evil which he had said that he would do to them, and he did it not. [Jon 3:10]

JONAS' VEXATION AND GOD'S ANSWER

There is someone who protests against this pardon—Jonas, the prophet. This, he thinks, is really too much:

And Jonas was exceedingly troubled and was angry.

And he prayed to Everlasting and said: "O Everlasting, is not this what I said when I was yet in my own country? Therefore I went before, to flee into Tharsis; for I know that you are a gracious and merciful God, patient and of much compassion and easy to forgive evil.

"And now, O Everlasting, I beseech you, take my life from me, for it is better for me to die than to live." [Jon 4:1-3]

This is a blunt way of saying it. Here, then, is the reason Jonas hesitated so long before accepting his mission. He knows God. God is ever the same: generous in grace and slow to anger, ever ready to forgive. We read into this passage the words used in the description of God's manifestation to Moses on Mount Sinai.[4]

This divine forgiveness is quite foreign to our human way of thinking. It represents a new type of justice—the justice of grace, the justice of God. Israel has once before been introduced to it in Second Isaias, where we find the concept of universalism and forgiveness outlined:

Assemble yourselves, and come, and draw together, you that are saved of the Gentiles. . . .

Am I not Everlasting, and there is no God else besides me? A just God and a savior. . . .

Be converted to me and you will be saved, all you ends of the earth, for I am God and there is no other. [Is 45:20-22]

But Jonas is thoroughly disheartened. He feels he is cutting a ridiculous figure in this whole affair. He was ordered to announce the coming of the punishment, and now the Ninevites are doing penance and no punishment has been meted out to them!

Everlasting said: "Do you think you have a reason to be angry?"

Then Jonas went out of the city, and sat toward the east side of the city; and he made himself a booth there, and he sat under it in the shade till he might see what would befall the city. [Jon 4:4-5]

Jonas pouts like a baby, very much as the elder brother does in the parable of the prodigal son. This worthy, too, is upset because the father has made a feast to celebrate the prodigal's return. In the evangelical parable, the father in his goodness goes out to his elder son and entreats him to share in his generosity and love (Lk 15:15-32). The same thing happens here. Has God not forgiven Jonas his earlier flight? He has forgiven Nineveh,

[4] See p. 37.

too. To forgive the repentant sinner is God's way. And God now wants to open the soul of Jonas, his prophet, his friend, to designs of divine intimacy. He does so in a kind of action parable.

And Everlasting prepared an ivy, and it came over the head of Jonas to be a shadow over his head and thus to relieve him.

And Jonas was exceedingly glad of the ivy.

But God prepared also a worm when the morning dawned on the following day, and it gnawed the ivy and it withered. And when the sun was risen Everlasting commanded a hot and burning wind, and the sun beat upon the head of Jonas and he broiled with the heat.

And he wished for death, saying: "It is better for me to die than to live." [Jon 4:6–8]

A little shade gives great joy; oppressive heat, a desire for death! Man is truly an overgrown baby! Thus does man's physical condition overwhelm his spirit.

These are all Oriental images: the hut built in haste of some palm leaves, very probably, spread over a pair of posts sunk in the sand; a man crouching beneath it waiting for the sun to set, lost in reverie; the plant gnawed by the worm; the sun; the parching desert wind.

There follows here a mild reproach, run through with some irony; but the irony too is mild, for it is God, now appearing on the desolate scene, who wields it:

And God said to Jonas: "Do you think you have a reason to be angry for the ivy?"

He answered: "I have a reason to be angry even unto death!"

Everlasting said: "You are grieved for the ivy, for which you have not labored, nor made it to grow, which in one night came up and in one night perished. And shall I not spare Nineveh, that great city, in which there are more than a hundred and twenty thousand persons that know not how to distinguish between their right hand and their left, as well as a great many beasts?" [Jon 4:9–11]

70

The contrast between man's cowardice and the immensity of God's mercy and the minute care he takes of every creature is enormous.

Such are the biblical circumstances of Jonas' forty days—a period of penance and prayer, of mercy and pardon, of conversion and divine love.

The Forty Years of the People of God in the Desert

IN the preceding chapters we have examined the forty-day symbol. This symbol now concerns an entire nation, and the forty days become forty years.

We are dealing here with the prodigiously busy time of the Exodus, the journey between two miraculous frontier water courses—the entry into the desert through the Red Sea and the exit from it through the River Jordan.

Viewed in this way, typologically, the forty years represent the whole of this earthly life, which is, in fact, a powerful action of God, a product of his grace terminating with the entry into the true Promised Land under the leadership of the true Josue: Jesus Christ. In general terms, this is a view that has been expressed by all the Fathers of the Church, and first of all by St. Paul.

I would not have you ignorant, brethren, that our fathers were all under the cloud and all passed through the sea; and all were baptized in Moses, in the cloud and in the sea. And all ate the same spiritual food and all drank the same spiritual drink (for they drank from the spiritual rock that followed them, and the rock was Christ). Yet with most of them God was not well pleased, for "they were laid low in the desert." ...

Now, all these things happened to them as a type, and they were written for our instruction, upon whom has come the final stage of the world. [1 Cor 10:1–5, 11]

Speaking to the Corinthians, Paul warns them of the danger of falling into idolatry. He is led incidentally to unfold this typological view of the forty years in the desert, beginning with a formula that, with him, always introduces an important message: "I would not have you ignorant, brethren. . . ."

Let us note here the difference between typology and allegory. Allegory, starting with Old Testament images or ideas or events, rises to considerations which often follow their own course. One who makes use of biblical allegory is undoubtedly conversant with the Bible and draws from all its riches to give expression to a religious idea. The connection, however, is often preserved between the literal reality that has served as a starting point and the idea that is developed therefrom. The biblical expression is employed as a means, a "body" for the concept one wishes to develop or the contemplation one wishes to achieve.

Typology, on the contrary, rests on a first reality that fits a kind of law of repetition. The fundamental historical reality in the Old Testament serves as a pattern for a renewed and deepened understanding of the significance of an event in the New Testament. This inner movement from one reality to another becomes then a divine pedagogy introducing us to the mystery.

In the above passage from the first Epistle to the Corinthians, Paul calls the journey through water and under the cloud (life and death—the Hebrews saved, the Egyptians destroyed) a baptism. He discovers in it a foreshadow of Christian baptism, an introduction to its profound significance. Again, in the miraculous food and drink he discovers a preparation for the eucharist. Even Christ, in fact, who is always the authentic typological link, emphasized this connection between manna and the eucharist in his speech on the bread of life. He also emphasized the relation between the water flowing from the rock and that rising unto life everlasting. We shall come back to this question presently.

Everlasting is called the "rock of Israel," that is, its protection, its strength, and its salvation. Paul applies the metaphor to Christ.

Origen uses a beautiful expression in reference to this concept of the "Christ-Rock." He begins by quoting Jesus' words to Peter: "I say to you that you are Peter, and on this Petra [rock] I will build my Church," and continues: "Simon is called a rock, receiving this name from the rock that is Christ, so that as 'wise' comes from 'wisdom' and 'saint' from 'sanctity,' so 'Peter' comes from 'Petra' " or rock.

In this passage from St. Paul, the forty years in the desert are characterized by the passage through the Red Sea, the manna, the water, and sin. All these elements contain lessons for us, says St. Paul, because they move toward us who move toward the end of time. Revelation has in fact come to its final completion: let no man add to the prophecy of this book, says St. John (Ap 22:18) The Church begins when Christ has fulfilled and perfected everything. She is but "the plenitude of Jesus Christ." With the first Easter morning begin the end of the world and the final consummation.

THE PASSAGE THROUGH THE SEA OF REEDS

The forty years in the desert are defined by two boundaries: the Red Sea and the River Jordan.[1]

The starting point to what St. Paul calls "the baptism of Moses" is the passage through the Sea of Reeds. It is not difficult to see that this biblical narrative is in an epic style. This does not weaken the force of its religious message; it delivers it with bare simplicity and thus strengthens it. A double literary tradition runs through the narrative: the Yahwist (God dams up the sea by the wind he raises; we are told of the reactions of the Egyptians) and the Priestly (Moses is portrayed as a mediator, the "theological" elements are well collected, etc.).

[1] Concerning the Passover from Egypt, see *Dieu Passe dans son Peuple* (Abbaye de Saint-André), and especially, regarding this whole chapter, see Auzou's *De la Servitude au Service* (Orante).

What are the facts of the situation as this sea crossing takes place?

The Hebrews, formed into groups (clans and families that have "left Egypt" on the night of the Passover), encamp apparently between the Bitter Lakes and the Gulf of Suez. Here we meet a multitude of people; there are Semites, but also foreigners, including some Egyptians (adventurers of various kinds). Now, after all the procrastination of the Pharaoh—during the crisis described in the story of the plagues of Egypt—the Egyptian army is in hot pursuit of the fugitives. At this point of the account, a few verses mention, as if in a resumé, what will eventually make the religious drama of the Exodus: the poor spiritual quality of the human herd God has chosen as his own People, the rebellions, the continual changing of sides, and, on the other hand, the firm attitude of Moses in the plenitude of his prophetic mission.

When Pharaoh drew near, the children of Israel, lifting up their eyes, saw the Egyptians behind them, and they feared exceedingly and cried toward Everlasting.

And they said to Moses: "Perhaps there were no graves in Egypt, that you have brought us to die in the wilderness. Why would you do this, to lead us out of Egypt? Is this not the word that we spoke to you in Egypt, saying: 'Depart from us that we may serve the Egyptians'—for it was much better to serve them than to die in the wilderness." [Ex 14:10–12]

It would be superfluous to try to explain these lines; they could not be clearer or more significant. We shall come upon some more of this blasphemous talk later on and shall examine it then.

Moses said to the people: "Fear not; stand and see the great wonders of Everlasting which he will do this day. For the Egyptians which you see now you will see no more forever. Everlasting will fight for you, and you will have nothing to do." [Ex 14:13–14]

Moses shines here as a man of faith, like Abraham of old. In this moment so tense with drama, he trusts blindly to the word of God.

In the following verses we find another metaphor from a different tradition: Moses' rod. This rod is his personal symbol. Moses is a shepherd. God has chosen him from among the flocks of Jethro, his father-in-law, to make him the shepherd of the People of Israel. Through the rod of this shepherd, Moses, God manifests his power to Israel and works signs and wonders.[2]

Everlasting said to Moses: "Why do you cry to me? Speak to the children of Israel to go forward. But lift up your rod and stretch your hand forth over the sea and divide it, so that the children of Israel may go through the midst of the sea on dry ground.

And I will harden the heart of the Egyptians to pursue you; and I shall cover myself with glory at the expense of Pharaoh and all his host and his chariots and his horsemen. And the Egyptians will know that I am Everlasting when I shall have covered myself with glory at the expense of Pharaoh and his chariots and his horsemen." [Ex 14:15–18]

What follows depends entirely on God; we see God's glory in it. This is an epic, but a religious epic, dealing with God's grace. Its whole style is "prophetic." Other religious images are drawn into the picture: first the angel, or God's messenger, which is a new way of expressing divine intervention; then the pillar of cloud. For the Hebrews the whole of creation is in the hollow of God's hand. He uses it as a means of expression, for it is ever at his beck and call.[3] In the passage we are about to quote, the

[2] In the same manner, the apostles who were fishermen will become fishers of men.

[3] For instance, in Ps 104:1–4, we read: "Everlasting, my God, you are exceedingly great: you have put on praise and beauty, and are clothed with light as with a garment; you have stretched out the heavens like a pavilion, and built your high chambers upon the waters; you have made the clouds your chariot, you walk upon the wings of the wind; you have made the winds your messengers, and your ministers a burning fire."

cloud is black at first. Then the sacred writer speaks of a strong easterly wind that carves a passage through the water. The children of Israel go through it, and while crossing they observe that the waters are dammed up on either side into a double wall.[4] At dawn the storm, announced by the black column already mentioned, breaks out into "a pillar of fire and of cloud." This may signify a torrential rain, lightning, and the reflux of the water as in a tidal wave. The Egyptians push through with their chariots, but the wheels stick in the mud. Confusion reigns as some try to force a passage forward while others are trying to go back. The result is disaster and general chaos. In the morning Israel can see the drowned bodies lying on the shore.

Israel has crossed the sea through the mercy of God, and is safe at last from its oppressor. Everlasting has covered himself with glory at the expense of Pharaoh, his chariots, and his horsemen. Can we not see in all this the genuine realism of religion, the true world of faith?

The angel of God who went before the camp of Israel changed places and went behind them.

And together with him the pillar of cloud, leaving the forepart, stood behind between the Egyptian camp and the camp of Israel; and it was a dark cloud, and the night went on without, throughout the night, the two armies being able to come close to each other.

Moses stretched out his hand over the sea. And Everlasting churned up the sea during the night by a strong easterly wind and turned it into dry ground. The waters were divided, and the children of Israel went in through the midst of the sea dried up; and the water was as a wall on their right hand and on their left.

The Egyptians, pursuing, went in after them—all Pharaoh's horses, his chariots and horsemen through the midst of the sea.

[4] We need not construct a childish picture of this, like for instance the scene in the film *The Ten Commandments*. The truth is at the same time more simple and more divine, more natural as well as more supernatural.

At dawn Everlasting, looking upon the Egyptian army through the pillar of fire and of the cloud, threw confusion into them. He sank their wheels, which could not advance except with the greatest difficulty.

And the Egyptians said: "Let us flee from Israel, for Everlasting fights with them against us."

Everlasting said to Moses: "Stretch forth your hand over the sea so that the waters may come again over the Egyptians, upon their chariots and horsemen."

Moses stretched forth his hand toward the sea, and it returned at break of day into its former place. And as the Egyptians were fleeing away, the waters came upon them, and Everlasting shut them up in the middle of the waves. The waters returning covered the chariots and the horsemen of all the army of Pharaoh, who had come into the sea after them; neither did so much as one of them remain.

But the children of Israel marched through the middle of the sea upon dry land, and the waters were to them as a wall on the right hand and on the left.

And Everlasting delivered Israel on that day out of the hands of the Egyptians; and they saw the Egyptians dead upon the seashore and the mighty hand that Everlasting had used against them.

And the people feared Everlasting and believed Everlasting and Moses, his servant. [Ex 14:19–31]

Notice how the passage ends—with an act of faith in God and trust in Moses. Israel has seen and can testify. Peter, in the same strain, will tell Cornelius the Centurion: "God has given to Jesus to be plainly seen . . . by witnesses designated beforehand by God . . . and he charged us to testify that he it is who has been appointed by God to be the judge of the living and of the dead" (Acts 10:41).

Religious tradition has interpreted this event as we have done, seeing in it God's intervention through his creation. Read, for example, these verses from the Psalms:

The waters saw you, O God, the waters saw you and they turned back and the depths were troubled. The clouds piled up the waters, the clouds sent out a sound, and your arrows flashed by.

The voice of the thunder rolled along; your lightnings enlightened the world, and the earth shook and trembled. Your way is in the sea, and your path in many waters, and your footsteps will not be known.

You have conducted your people like sheep by the hand of Moses and Aaron. [Ps 77:17–21]

The crossing of the Red Sea has left an indelible mark on sacred history. Before going through the water, the People were afraid to die; but it is in the water that they found their new life, their life as the People of God, and with it their vocation, their freedom, and a path to the Land of Promise:

He divided the Red Sea into two parts, for his mercy endures forever. He brought out Israel through the midst thereof, for his mercy endures forever. And he overthrew Pharaoh and his host, for his mercy endures forever. [Ps 136:13–15]⁵

To St. Paul, at the end of this tradition, the passage through the Red Sea typifies, as we have seen, Christian baptism: "I would not have you ignorant, brethren, that our fathers were all under the cloud and all passed through the sea; and all were baptized in Moses, in the cloud and in the sea. . . . And all these things happened to serve us as a type . . ." (1 Cor 1–2, 6). Father Auzou, in his excellent work on the Exodus, offers this comment:

Christ, too, had to pass through death to come to his Resurrection. "All of us who have been plunged [literal sense of the verb *to baptize*] into Christ Jesus have been plunged into his death. We have been buried with him by our descent [baptism] into death, in order

⁵ See also Ps 114 (Sunday vespers), which celebrates this event with a great sense of triumph; and see also Is 63:11–13, a great psalm written at the end of the Exile with deep spiritual inspiration, telling us what this sea crossing represented in the religious tradition of the People in exile.

that, just as Christ has arisen from the dead by the power of his Father, so we also may walk in newness of life" (Rom 6:3–4). This explains why baptism has found its appropriate place in the liturgy of the Paschal vigil.[6]

THE FORTY–YEAR PUNISHMENT

What is the real meaning of this forty-year sojourn in the desert, then? It is twofold: a time of chastisement and tribulation,[7] but also a time of purification and regeneration—a period of grace and of active divine presence.

In the Book of Numbers the forty-year sojourn is explicitly linked with another distinct period of forty days.

After the Exodus from Egypt and the first retreat on Mount Sinai that ended with the proclamation of the Covenant, and perhaps after the People have encamped at the oasis of Cades, Moses sends scouts to explore the land of Canaan. Everything now seems ready for their entry into the Promised Land.

Everlasting spoke to Moses, saying: "Send men to view the land of Canaan which I will give to the children of Israel, the princes of every tribe."

Moses did what Everlasting had commanded, sending from the desert of Pharan principal men whose names are these:

Of the tribe of Ruben, Sammua, the son of Zechur.
Of the tribe of Simeon, Saphat, the son of Huri.
Of the tribe of Judah, Caleb, the son of Jephone.
Of the tribe of Issachar, Igal, the son of Joseph.
Of the tribe of Ephraim, Osee, the son of Nun.
Of the tribe of Benjamin, Phalti, the son of Raphu.
Of the tribe of Zabulon, Geddiel, the son of Sodi.
Of the tribe of Joseph, for the tribe of Manasses, Gaddi, the son of Susi.

---

[6] Auzou, *op. cit.,* pp. 207–208.

[7] See the chapter *"Carême et Pentecôte"* in Father Daniélou's *Essai sur le mystère de l'Histoire* (Seuil).

Of the tribe of Dan, Ammiel, the son of Gemalli.
Of the tribe of Aser, Sthur, the son of Michael.
Of the tribe of Nephtali, Nahabi, the son of Vapsi.
Of the tribe of Gad, Guel, the son of Machi.

These are the names of the men whom Moses sent to view the land; and he called Osee, the son of Nun, Josue. [Nm 13:1-17]

What interest do these names hold for us? They are the names of the delegates of the people. Through them the whole of Israel carries out a first exploration of the land "which I will give," says God, "to the children of Israel."

Osee is given a new name. We know the symbolic importance of the name Osee throughout the Bible, from the Old to the New Testament: Osee means "save."[8] Josue means "Yahweh saves" or "God saves." This is the name the angel will ask Mary to give to her son: "You will call him Jesus" (Mt 1:21, Lk 1:31).

These scouts cross the Desert of Sin, then the Negeb, and traverse the whole of Palestine right up to the Hemat Desert; and the exploration takes forty days. Here we are again with the biblical forty. The forty-day period never ends within that time; no stable or fixed duration is denoted by this symbol. It only stands for a period of preparation and expectation. Pending the final entry of the whole People into the Land of Promise, these representatives are, as it were, first fruits; also, they will take the first fruits of the land back with them to the desert where the children of Israel are encamped.

Now it was the time when the first ripe grapes are fit to be eaten. . . . And going forward as far as the valley of Eskol, they cut off a branch with its cluster of grapes, which two men carried upon a pole; they took also of the pomegranates and of the figs of that place.

They called this place the valley of Eskol because of the bunch of grapes which the children of Israel had cut in it. [Nm 13:21, 24-25]

[8] Hence the cry "Hosanna," that is, "Save!"

Grapes, figs, and pomegranates: this is indeed Palestine! This valley of Eskol (which means a bunch of grapes) is near Hebron. The two men carrying the grapes have served as the subject of cathedral sculptures and illuminations in missals and manuscripts.

Thus, while the People in the desert are living on manna, the explorers are tasting the riches of the land that flows with milk and honey. The report they make at the end of their forty-day exploration is unanimous as to the fertility of the soil, but about the possibility of conquering the country all but two, Josue and Caleb, are quite pessimistic. The explorers have not been thinking as men "called from on high" and "saved by God," but are seeing only the "natural" appearances of things. The proposed enterprise is for them only a human venture. Looked at from this point of view, the undertaking is, of course, unpromising. Thus, the People of God are disheartened and rebel.

They that went to explore the land returned after forty days. And they came to Moses and Aaron and to all the assembly of the children of Israel to the desert of Pharan, which is in Cades. And speaking to them and to all the multitude, they showed them the fruits of the land.

And they related and said: "We came into the land to which you sent us, which indeed does flow with milk and honey, as may be known by these fruits; but it has very strong inhabitants, and the cities are great and walled. . . ."

And they spoke ill of the land which they had explored before the children of Israel, saying: "The land which we have viewed devours its inhabitants. The people that we beheld are of a tall stature. There we saw certain monsters of the sons of Enac, of the giant kind, in comparison to whom we seemed like locusts."

Therefore the whole multitude cried out, and in the night people wept.

And all the children of Israel murmured against Moses and Aaron, saying: "Would that we had died in Egypt! and would that we may die in this vast wilderness, and that Everlasting may not bring us into this land, lest we fall by the sword and our wives and children be led away captives. Is it not better to return into Egypt?

And they said to one another: "Let us appoint a captain, and let us return into Egypt." [Nm 13:26–29, 33–34; 14:1–4]

So this is the effect of the forty-day exploration—people grumbling and blaspheming against the love of God! God has saved them from servitude with a strong hand and an extended arm; he has carved out a passage for them through the Red Sea; he has made a Covenant with them and given them his law; he has fed them and given them drink and defended them, and has not cut them down for their lack of faith—and at heart, they are still in Egypt. They reject Moses; but infinitely more serious, they deny God. What is to be done? Moses and Aaron think only of God and prostrate themselves on the ground, their face in the dust. Josue and Caleb, the only brave and faithful ones among the scouts, adjure the people to have trust in God:

And when Moses and Aaron heard this, they fell down flat upon the ground before the multitude of the children of Israel.

But Josue, the son of Nun, and Caleb, the son of Jephone, who also had viewed the land, rent their garments, and said to all the multitude of the children of Israel: "The land we have seen is very good. If Everlasting be favorable, he will bring us into it and give us a land flowing with milk and honey. Be not rebellious against Everlasting; and yet fear not the people of this land, for we can eat them up in one mouthful. Their protecting shadow has forsaken them, but Everlasting is with us. Have no fear." [Nm 14:5–9]

One thing to be noted in this text is the repetition of the expression "the multitude of the children of Israel." It is the People as an entity that is involved, the People as the God-chosen community. The essential, say Josue and Caleb, is not to rebel against God. The pagan idols are called a "shadow." Ahead is "Emmanuel"—God-with-us.

Here we have again the dialogue and the intercessory power of prayer. God manifests himself, reminds his people of their sin, and decrees the punishment:

And when all the multitude cried out and would have stoned them [Josue and Caleb], the glory of Everlasting appeared over the Meeting Tent to all the children of Israel. And Everlasting said to Moses: "How long will this people despise me? How long will they not believe in me in spite of all the signs that I have wrought before them? I will strike them therefore with pestilence and will consume them. But of thee I will make a ruler over a great nation and a mightier than this is." [Nm 14:10–12]

The Meeting Tent is the same tent, described above, built outside the camp for intercourse with God.

The people should have believed because of the signs. This is precisely the reproach of Jesus to his contemporaries: "Why do you not believe in my signs?" ("in my works," he actually said).

God proposes to destroy the people and make a fresh start. To this Moses replies with a typical request. He recalls God's benefits and the testimonial nature these benefits have in the eyes of all nations; he recalls in a special manner the revelation God gave him on Sinai which will forever mark his understanding of God.

And Moses said to Everlasting:

"But the Egyptians have learned that by your strength you have brought forth this people from their midst. They have repeated it to the inhabitants of this land. They know that you, O Everlasting, are among this people and are seen face to face,[9] and your cloud protects them, and you go before them in a pillar of cloud by day and in a pillar of fire by night.[10] If you kill this people as one man, the nations that have heard speak of you will say: 'Everlasting could not

[9] We have seen that it is not really so. No one can look on God without dying. The People have seen only the presence of God in the wonders mentioned in the text.

[10] See p. 116.

bring the people into the land for which he had sworn; therefore did he kill them in the wilderness.'

"Let then the strength of Everlasting be shown according to your promise, that 'Everlasting is patient and full of mercy'. . . . Forgive, I beseech you, the sins of this people according to the greatness of your mercy, as you have been merciful to them from their going out of Egypt unto this place." [Nm 14:13–19]

Prayer overcomes sin. God will not completely destroy this People, but will regenerate it during a long wandering in the desert. The exploration of the Promised Land took forty days; this wandering will last forty years! Those among the People who are more than twenty years old will die during this great quarantine, except the two faithful scouts, who will be as a remnant of those who came out of Egypt. All the People will be new, raised in the desert. Such is God's revised verdict:

Everlasting said: "I have forgiven [the People] according to your word. But as I live, and as the glory of Everlasting will fill the whole earth, all the men that have seen my majesty and the signs that I have done in Egypt and in the wilderness, and have tempted me now ten times and have not obeyed my voice, will not see the land for which I swore to their fathers, nor will any of them that have despised me behold it. . . .

"As I live, I, Everlasting! According as you have spoken in my hearing, so will I do to you.

"In the wilderness will your carcasses lie. All of you that are more than twenty years old and have murmured against me will not enter into the land over which I lifted up my hand to make you dwell therein, except Caleb, the son of Jephone, and Josue, the son of Nun.

"But your children, of whom you said that they might be a prey to the enemy, will I bring in, that they may see the land which you have despised.

"Your carcasses will lie in the wilderness. Your children will wander in the desert forty years, and will bear the burden of your infidelity, until the carcasses of their fathers be all accounted for in the desert.

"According to the number of the forty days wherein you explored the land, a year will be counted for a day. And forty years you will receive your iniquities; and you will learn what it means to forsake me. Thus I, Everlasting, have spoken."[11] [Nm 14:20–23, 28–35]

THE FORTY YEARS OF GRACE
AND PREPARATION

The wandering in the desert is first of all a chastisement and a trial, and we shall have to retain this meaning. But it is not the only meaning—there is another and more important aspect: grace, God's presence, God's operation.

The arrival in the desert has been an astonishing act of deliverance; the Jews have been "baptized" in the Red Sea, as St. Paul puts it. The religious canticle commemorating the event signals it as a marvelous intervention of God:

I sing to Everlasting: he has covered himself with glory; the horse and the rider he has thrown into the sea.

Everlasting is my strength and my song: he has become a salvation to me.

He is my God, and I glorify him; the God of my fathers, and I exalt him. [Ex 15:1–2]

This dispensation of grace is treated in all the liturgy of Israel. Thus, the great Hallel psalm,[12] sung in the celebration of the Pasch, says: "[He] led his people through the desert, for his mercy endures forever" (Ps 136:16), which Deuteronomy, written

[11] The theme of the forty years of chastisement is resumed in Ez 29 in a prophecy against Egypt: "Thus says Everlasting: '. . . the land of Egypt will become a desert and a wilderness, and they will know that I am Everlasting,' for he has said: 'Mine is the Nile I made it. Therefore, I now come against you and your Niles, and I will make the land of Egypt utterly desolate . . . nor shall it be inhabited during forty years'" (Ez 29:9–11). See Daniélou, op. cit., p. 249.

[12] See p. 109, n. 23.

under a prophetic influence, echoes: "Everlasting, your God, has blessed you in every work of your hands; he has watched over you when you did go through this great wilderness for forty years, and you have wanted nothing" (Dt 2:7). Thus also Amos: "'It is I,' says Everlasting, 'that brought you up out of the land of Egypt, and I led you for forty years through the wilderness'" (Amos 2:10). The tone gathers intensity with Jeremias:

Thus says Everlasting: "I remember the love of your youth, the love of your espousals, when you followed me in the desert, in a land that is not sown. Israel was holy to Everlasting, the first fruits of his harvest. . . ." [Jer 2:2–3]

The sojourn in the desert is thus the betrothal of the Covenant. And when the People of Israel finally settle in the Land of Promise and again prove unfaithful by following "vanities," that is, false gods, the last means God will resort to to bring them back and to gain a love more beauteous still than the first will consist in taking the People back to the desert:

Therefore I will allure her, and will lead her into the wilderness, and I will speak to her heart.

. . . and she shall sing there as in the days of her youth, as in the days when she came up from the land of Egypt. [Hos 2:14–15]

This, then, is the second aspect of this forty-year stay in the desert: it is a blessed time. At the end the remnant of Israel, saved, purified, prepared, will be worthy to enter the Promised Land. When this event takes place, therefore, Josue and Caleb, the two faithful scouts of the first exploration, will play the role that Noah played after the Deluge. They will be the living witnesses of God's grace, the instruments that make it possible for God to bring his designs to completion and link the present with the past.

In the passage from the Epistle to the Corinthians that we

quoted at the beginning of this chapter, Paul underscores on the double typological gift of this forty-year period: the manna and the water from the rock.

THE MANNA

The manna is the viaticum, the bread-for-the-road of these forty years. Its symbolic significance is that God would impress us with the necessity of depending patiently and completely on him alone in all things, beginning with our physical life.[13] The act he expects of man's free will is utter abandonment to his providence. This, precisely, is what the first man refused him. As a basic ingredient in our learning this lesson anew, little by little, we have this fundamental requirement for life which our animal natures cannot help recognizing as an urgent need: our daily bread.

This earthly life is of overpowering concern even to people who seldom think about it. Hunger creates a void that craves for nourishment, and the food that symbolizes all nourishment is bread. This bread must be earned by man "with the sweat of his brow": ". . . cursed is the earth in your work; with labor and toil will you eat thereof all the days of your life. . . . In the sweat of your brow you will eat your bread" (Gn 3:17, 19).

In this laborious fight for bread man should discover the connection between his own persevering efforts and the gratuitous largess of the all-powerful Provider. When the cultivator has done with plowing, sowing, perspiring, his face bent to the soil, he turns anxious eyes to him who alone dispenses "rains from heaven and fruitful seasons" (Acts 14:16). The grain buried in the ground dies (Jn 12:24), but out of it a new blade sprouts and grows without the sower's knowing how. First comes the blade,

[13] See Roger Poelman, "*Le Pain de route*," *Maison-Dieu*, no. 18.

then the stem, and then the ear laden with grain (Mk 14:27-28). The Creator lavishes abundance of nourishment and fills all hearts with joy. Human toil and divine grace—"Nothing is left but to wield the sickle, for the harvest is ready"—produces the bread for man's journey, our daily bread.

This dependence on God for each day's bread is an object lesson all men have learned. The way they express this knowledge may be bizarre at times (as in the harvest ceremonies of witch doctors), but it is always meaningful.

It was God's design that this dependence, implied in the very nature of bread as a requisite for life, should be manifested in a special manner to his own People, the People of Israel. Let us see how he did it.

The sixteenth chapter of Exodus has its origin mainly in the Priestly tradition. This is evident chiefly in the emphasis it lays on the Sabbath.

The scene opens on the People grumbling. They have marched some weeks in the desert since their liberation from Egypt and have passed through the Red Sea, and fatigue begins to tell on them; they are hungry, and the provisions are exhausted. What will become of them, this rather disorganized multitude? Then:

All the congregation of the children of Israel murmured against Moses and Aaron in the wilderness. . . . "Would to God we had died by the hand of Everlasting in the land of Egypt when we sat over the flesh pots and ate bread to the full. Why have you brought us into the desert, that you might destroy all the multitude with famine?" [Ex 16:2-3]

Hardly are the People freed before they begin to miss their past servitude because of the material goods it gave them. Obviously, they have not yet acquired a sense of direction; they cannot as yet walk in hope toward the Land of Promise. They have not yet learned from the wonders that have already taken place how to trust in God. We come here to an important moment in God's pedagogy. Something happens when the provisions brought from Egypt fail. There is nothing at all now that man can do; the time has come for him to look above for help. Let all nations see what "he who is" can do for his own:

Everlasting said to Moses: "Behold, I will rain bread from heaven for you; let the people go forth and gather what is sufficient for every day that I may prove them, whether they will walk in my law or not." [Ex 16:4]

The Priestly writer describes the whole scene as if the People were already within the Temple; and this approach, if not in historic perspective, introduces us nevertheless to a profound reality: the events taking place in the desert are the beginnings of a liturgy, even though the People themselves perhaps do not realize it. The God to be worshiped in the Temple is none other than he who feeds his people in the wilderness. (In the same way, in the Paschal liturgy, the last supper is prepared in the Cenacle by the same Christ who has multiplied loaves in a desert place by a lake.)

Moses said to Aaron: "Say to the multitude of the children of Israel, 'Come before Everlasting, for he has heard your murmuring.'"

And when Aaron spoke to all the assembly of the children of Israel, they looked toward the wilderness, and behold, the glory of Everlasting appeared in a cloud.

". . . in the morning you will have your fill of bread, and you will know that I am Everlasting, your God." [Ex 16:9–10]

On the following morning (that biblical morning, the time of God's purest graces), as the People peep out of their tents, they are filled with amazement:

90

There was, on the face of the wilderness, something small, and as it were beaten with a pestle, like the hoar frost on the ground. And they said to one another, "Man hu?" which signifies, "What is this?" Moses said to them: "This is the bread that Everlasting is giving you to eat." [Ex 16:14–16]

What is this manna, actually? No one knows. Some authors suggest that it is the white gum produced by a kind of tamarisk. The sign, in any case, is this: God's People have now received a food which they were not counting on, received it from God; and because of it they are able to proceed toward the Promised Land. Everlasting has spread a table for his own People in the desert. He feeds them, day after day, with this heavenly nourishment, this "bread of the strong," as the psalmist calls it (Ps 78:23–25). In God's plan, this manna will fall afresh every day: "Let every one collect one gomor each" (a three-quart jar), one gomor and no more: this is God's repast, and it suffices for the day. Above all, let there be no storing up. One gomor each morning—some who had accumulated more saw it destroyed by maggots. Moreover, at sunrise, whatever was left of the manna turned to water.

This is how the Bible, in its final written form, presents the episode of the manna. The man who tries to settle the future will lose his bearings; he runs the risk of stalling. Christ will condemn this calculating attitude, so contrary to the spirit of the Gospel, in one of his parables:

The land of a certain rich man brought forth abundant crops. And he began to take thought within himself, saying: "What shall I do for I have no room to store my crops?" And he said: "I will do this: I will pull down my barns and build larger ones, and there I will store up all my grain and my goods. And I say to my soul: 'Soul, you have many good things laid up for many years; take your ease, eat, drink, and be merry.'" [Lk 12:16–21]

We hear the words of this man to his soul, and his attitude is obvious. He relies on himself for the future. He is self-sufficient and quite at ease. He appropriates the future to himself, trusting in his grain.

But he hardly has the time to do so. God breaks in on the rustic scene like a tempest, like a thunderclap in a summer sky. "You fool! This night do they demand your soul of you!"—this soul that should have kept its sense of direction, accepted dependence on God! It is only on the seventh day here below and on the eighth in the future life that we can eat the bread of God in peace and sit at his eternal wedding banquet.

In fact, the Israelites are allowed to gather a double ration of manna on the sixth day, for the following day is a special one, a prelude to the great heavenly rest. With this detail the Priestly writer emphasizes to the People of God the importance of the Sabbath.

The children of Israel are nourished with manna for forty years, until they arrive at the border of the land of Canaan. They cross the Jordan then and pitch their tents at Gilgal; and toward evening on the fourteenth day of the month, in the plains of Jericho, they celebrate the Passover, their first Pasch in the Land of Promise. The rejoicing that accompanies the feast is easy to imagine. (Think, by way of contrast, of the first Passover, celebrated in Egypt in the anxious and decisive hours of the fateful departure.) And the manna ceases the day after their arrival—thus runs the text, as it has come down to us, with all its significant insistence. The wanderings are finished now; ended is the bread of the desert; the destination has finally been reached (Jos 5:10-12).

This dependence on God, symbolized for all men in their daily bread and emphasized in this manna which Everlasting has given his people without their having worked for it, like the food of the little birds that neither sow nor reap but of which the heavenly Father takes care (Mt 6:26), introduces the revelation of another dependence more fundamental still:

He afflicted you with want, and gave you manna for your food, which neither you nor your fathers knew, to show that not in bread alone does a man live, but in every word that proceeds from the mouth of Everlasting. [Dt 8:3]

"Behold, the days come," says Everlasting, "and I will send forth a famine into the land, not a famine of bread but of hearing the word of Everlasting." [Amos 8:11]

And now let us listen to this word of God repeated by the Word made flesh, Jesus Christ, who reveals to us at last the innermost meaning of this bread-for-the-road. He tells us what it is that God foreshadowed by providing the harvests of the fields and the manna of the sky. He reveals to us the mystery of the holy eucharist.

The discourse on the bread of life is found in the sixth chapter of the Gospel of St. John. This discourse is directly connected with the miracle of the multiplication of the loaves. A large crowd is assembled in a desert spot and there is nothing to eat, a fact that distresses the apostles. Christ gives thanks to the Father, publicly and solemnly as in a liturgy, and, as a lord entertaining his guests, multiplies the breads and entrusts them to the apostles to be distributed to the people. The crowd, astonished, cries out: "This is indeed the Prophet that is to come into the world" (Jn 6:14). The Jews awaited the Messiah, who was to be a new Moses and who would renew the miracles of the Exodus.[14]

What is the message of this Prophet? The people make a search for him after he has left them, and find him at Capharnaum.

[14] See p. 35, n. 3.

. . . you seek me not because you have seen signs [the signs that draw men's attention to another world], but because you have eaten of the loaves and have been filled.

Do not labor for the food that perishes but for that which endures unto life everlasting which the Son of man will give you. [Jn 6:26–27]

"Then, Lord, what have we to do?"

"Believe in him whom God has sent."

Believe, for the bread that is being revealed is a mystery of faith. Jesus, this new envoy of God, reminds us of Moses, God's great messenger sent for the deliverance of the People of the Old Testament, the man of the Passover, the prophet who introduces the manna of the desert. The Jews notice the analogy immediately, and say: "What sign, then, do you do . . . ? Our fathers ate the manna in the desert. . . ." Jesus replies: "Moses did not give you the bread from heaven, but my Father [God] gives you the true bread from heaven. For the bread of God is that which comes down from heaven [from God] and gives life to the world [of men]" (Jn 6:30–33).

"I am the bread of life," he continues. To the Samaritan woman he promises the living water (Jn 4:10–14). "He was the life of all things," says St. John's Prologue concerning the Word of God (Jn 1:4).

He who comes to me will not hunger, and he who believes in me will never thirst. . . .

I am the bread of life. Your fathers ate the manna in the desert and have died. This is the bread that comes down from heaven, so that if anyone eat of it he will not die. [Jn 6:35, 48–50]

Jesus has multiplied the loaves in the desert, and the crowd has followed him. Is sacred history repeating itself? No; it is being fulfilled. For himself and for the People who will depend on him, Jesus reviews the religious characteristics of that manna of the forty-year journey. We have seen how man must depend on God, how man must be fed by God. We shall see now to what extraordinary lengths this dependence must be carried and what privileges it involves.

I am the living bread that has come down from heaven. If anyone eat of this bread, he will live forever. And the bread that I will give is my flesh for the life of the world. [Jn 6:51]

This is no longer simply the food of the desert; it is the flesh of Christ that will be given, surrendered, sacrificed for the life of the world. The Jews are scandalized; their human comprehension is completely baffled.

The Jews . . . argued with one another, saying: "How can this man give us his flesh to eat?"

Jesus therefore said to them: "Amen, amen, I say to you; unless you eat the flesh of the Son of man and drink his blood, you will not have life in you.

"He who eats my flesh and drinks my blood has life everlasting, and I will raise him up on the last day.

"For my flesh is food indeed and my blood is drink indeed." [Jn 6:53–56]

Instead of explaining his meaning, Jesus repeats and insists: this new food and drink which the new Moses dispenses to God's new People is really his own flesh and blood. It confers eternal life and the resurrection of the new Passover. It brings about a new Exodus.

And what marvelous dependence will this manna establish between Christ and those who receive it?

He who eats my flesh and drinks my blood abides in me and I in him.

As the living Father has sent me, and as I live because of the Father, so he who eats me, he also will live because of me. [Jn 6:57–58]

95

That is it: receiving the new manna will make us depend on Christ for everything, in the same manner as Christ himself lives in complete dependence on his Father. To describe the nature of the life of those who receive manna, Christ finds no better comparison than that of his own life with the Father.

With the strength drawn from this manna, the People of Jesus can reach the Land of Promise. Then they will receive it one last time as a viaticum, a food-for-the-journey, and they will cross the dividing line and live forever.

"This is the bread that has come down from heaven, not as your fathers ate the manna and died: he who eats this bread will live forever."

These things he said when teaching in the synagogue at Capharnaum. [Jn 6:59–60]

The apostles will not fully understand the sign embodied in the multiplication of the loaves or the discourse at Capharnaum until they sit around the table of the last supper.

No one describes the institution of the supper better than St. Paul in the Epistle to the Corinthians from which we quoted at the beginning of this chapter and in which he refers to events in the desert.

I myself have received from the Lord that which I have in turn delivered to you.

The Lord Jesus, on the night on which he was betrayed, took bread and, giving thanks, broke, and said:

"This is my body which shall be given up for you. Do this in remembrance of me." [1 Cor. 11:23–24]

The apostles were intimately connected with the miracle of the multiplication of the loaves since they themselves distributed the bread to the crowd. They also heard Christ's discourse at Capharnaum, and sat down with him at the last supper. They now perform again the action of their Lord, and as they repeat his words they come to a clear understanding, one that is rich and so mysterious, divine and yet so human too, of the manna of the forty years.

THE WATER OF THE ROCK

Another sign of the benevolence of Everlasting, typical of the graces of the forty years in the desert, is the water flowing from the rock. The echo of this episode is heard again and again in tradition, and we find its mysterious fulfillment in the Gospels.

Here are the details as narrated in Exodus.

As soon as the People set foot on the path of freedom after crossing the Red Sea, they are tempted and tried by Everlasting at the waters of Mara.

The People of Israel, at the command of Moses, removed their camp from near the Sea of Reeds, and went forth into the wilderness of Sur, and they marched three days through the wilderness and they found no water.

And they came to Mara, but could not drink the water of that place because it was bitter: hence the name "Mara" [bitter] given to the place.

And the People murmured against Moses, saying: "What shall we drink?" Moses then cried to Everlasting, and Everlasting showed him a kind of wood. When Moses threw this into the water, this became sweet.

. . . this is the place where God tried them. . . . [Ex 15:22–26]

We have here, in a few words, a typical example of the relations among the People, Moses, and God during these forty years.[15] Humanly speaking, the situation is very difficult indeed.

[15] Dt 9:24 says a terrible thing: "You have rebelled against Everlasting from the first day he has known you."

Imagine this march through the torrid, waterless desert. Think of the joy of at last finding a spring—followed by a cruel disappointment: the water is not potable; it is bitter!

The People's immediate, crudely natural reaction reveals an utter lack of faith and hope—exactly as if God did not exist, as if he had done nothing as yet to manifest his love. And all the blame falls on the mediator, Moses.

Then, in contrast, we have Moses, the man who from the beginning has understood the burdens involved in his mission and done his best to decline them (Ex 4:1–17); Moses who, here in the desert, has only one helper, only one whom he can consult and from all assistance must come: Everlasting.[16]

And in this relationship God always comes to the rescue.

Now the People come to Raphidim, a valley in the Sinai mountain range, and water fails again. A loosely organized crowd of men, women, and children, without counting the beasts of burden and the flocks, is assembled on the desert.

The People then chided Moses, saying: "Give us water that we may drink."

And Moses answered them: "Why do you chide me? Why do you tempt Everlasting?"

So the people were thirsty for want of water and murmured against Moses, saying: "Why did you make us go forth out of the land Egypt, to kill us and our children and our beasts with thirst?"

And Moses cried to Everlasting, saying: "What shall I do to this people? Yet a little more and they will stone me."

Everlasting said to Moses: "Go before the people and take with you of the ancients of Israel; and take in your hand the rod wherewith you did strike the river, and go. Behold, I will stand there before you upon the rock Horeb. You will strike the rock, and water will come out of it that the people may drink."

Moses did so before the ancients of Israel.

[16] See p. 76.

And he called the name of that place Massah and Meribah because of the quarrel sought by the children of Israel and because they tempted Everlasting, saying: "Is Everlasting with us, or is he not?" [Ex 17:1–7]

This last question sounds like a threat, but it also contains a touching undertone: Everlasting has assisted us once before at Mara; let him give us water again!

Let us visualize what the desert means to these people on the march. They have tramped for hours under a pitiless sun and have seen nothing but sand and rocks or, in the Sinai peninsula, those enormous cliffs, chaotic, sometimes red-tinted, extraordinarily beautiful against a monotonously blue sky, set in that play of light and shadow that gives the valleys unusual hues of pink, brown-yellow, and opal. They have seen all this, and at times, perhaps, a thorny acacia tree, but not one blade of grass and not one drop of water. And so they suffer hour after hour of parched tongues and gnawing thirst until, finally, they are utterly exhausted. Children whine and moan and have to be carried. They march on, without knowing where to. Nothing they can see affords any hope.

All the ugly human instincts well up within their hearts— anger and rebellion, forgetfulness of everything that in the past has been good and happy, selfishness, blasphemy. In the second and seventh verses of the Hebrew original, the word *rib*—to pick a quarrel, hence Meribah—occurs three times. Another word is used twice: *nasah* in Hebrew, that is, to tempt, to put to the test. The names Massah and Meribah are given to this place, as Mara was the name given to the spring sweetened by Moses.

The quarrel with Moses is aggravated by the unjust taunt: you delivered us from Egypt to make us die in the desert. Such is the mob! They are thirsty and lose their self-control. They threaten to stone their chief to death.

Their tempting God, putting him to the test, claiming rights from him practically means denying his grace and rejecting dependence on him. He is reviled and treated as a mere human being. There is no surrender to his will any longer.

"Is Everlasting with us, or is he not?"[17]

This tragic question is quite understandable. The prophets themselves will ask it on the spur of harrowing tribulations. The sigh of the sufferer, "My God, my God! why have you forsaken me?" must touch God's heart deeply. But what a sin when God is thus challenged, tempted, defied!

Against all this human weakness, we observe the sovereign attitude of God and hear his reply.

A rock dominates the scene. It is like a huge mass in their path, without a crack or a pass. These details are intended to emphasize the extraordinary nature of God's intervention. Decidedly, the rock holds no water. But the rock is also a symbol of might and permanence. In a spiritual sense it signifies protection, assurance, and rest; and in this sense *Rock* will become one of the People's names for Everlasting.

Moses is told to proceed to the rock, rod in hand—the same rod mentioned in connection with the passage across the Red Sea.[18] Some of the ancients of Israel station themselves nearby as appointed witnesses and God takes his place on the rock itself, opposite Moses. The whole scene is enacted before God, that is, in his presence. At the command of God, Moses strikes the rock, and water gushes forth in a great stream.[19]

[17] In the Book of Judith (chaps. 7 and 8), we find another typical God-sent trial and with it the *correct* spiritual reaction of the truly faithful soul.

[18] See p. 71.

[19] The Book of Numbers (20:11) gives us an account similar to or perhaps identical with this Exodus passage.

All now can drink to their heart's content. With this water life starts anew, bodies relax, souls are appeased, joy returns. Brothers come together again, conversation is resumed, and no doubt songs are heard, too. This gushing stream is the gift of God.

The transgression and the grace of Massah and Meribah have been carefully remembered in the religious tradition of Israel. In the great prayer recorded in sacred history, this gift of the water from the rock is celebrated in enthusiastic words: "He struck the rock in the wilderness and gave them to drink, as out of a great deep; he brought forth water out of the rock, and streams ran down as rivers" (Ps 78:15–16).[20] But a vivid remembrance has been retained of the transgression, too:

They added yet more sin against God; they provoked him to wrath in the desert. And they tempted God in their hearts. . . .

They spoke ill of God, saying: "Can God furnish a table in the wilderness?" And behold! He struck a rock and the waters gushed out, and the streams overflowed. . . . [Ps 78:17–20]

In the Book of Isaias there is a short little poem of uncertain date that speaks of the appeased anger of God and the joyous gift of the saving waters. The Church takes up the last two verses and uses them in celebrating the Feast of the Sacred Heart.

You will say in that day: I will give thanks to you, Everlasting, for you were angry with me; your wrath is turned away, and you have comforted me.

Behold, God is my savior; I will be confident and will not fear because Everlasting is my strength and my song; he is become my salvation.
You will draw waters with joy out of the saving fountains. . . . [Is 12:1–3]

[20] See also Is 48:21.

A characteristic psalm, Psalm 95, is devoted to the rebellion at Massah and Meribah. It is a processional hymn, probably sung during the Feast of the Tabernacles when the great miracles of the Exodus were commemorated.[21] We shall come back to this feast, which assumes its full significance during the life of Christ. Deuteronomy says in allusion to it, "In the feast of the tabernacles, when all Israel come together to appear in the sight of Everlasting, your God, in the place which he will choose . . ." (Dt 31:11). This spiritual allusion fully conveys the spirit of the psalm:

Come, let us praise Everlasting with joy; let us joyfully sing to the Rock of salvation.

Let us come before his presence with thanksgiving, and make a joyful noise to him with psalms. [Ps 95:1–2]

The title used for Everlasting, "the Rock of salvation," reminds us of the rock of Meribah gushing forth waters to save the children of Israel. The remembrance of this miracle of grace has come down from father to son and is now introduced into the chants of the liturgy. The Rock of Israel reminds us, too, of the field of Areuna the Jebusite, which David bought and on which Solomon built the Temple. Thus the Temple rested on the Rock, the most elevated place in Jerusalem. There, in the presence of Everlasting, on the site he had chosen, people gathered during the procession of the Feast of the Tabernacles. We must underline the significance of this liturgy of Priestly origin but also so simple and so much of the people: "Come, let us praise Everlasting with joy!"

[21] On the subject of this feast, see Dom Thierry Mærtens' interesting work *C'est fête en l'honneur d'Éternel* (Desclée), pp. 57–77, and Father Jean Daniélou's article *"Le symbolisme eschatologique de la Fête des Tabernacles,"* *Irenikon,* XXXI (first quarter, 1958), 19–40.

For Everlasting is a great God, and a great king above all gods.

In his hands are all the ends of the earth, and the heights of the mountains are his. The sea is his, and he made it, and his hands formed the dry land. [vv. 3–5]

Everlasting is a king without compare, above all Canaanite gods and pagan divinities. He reigns over the world through his creating power. This thought is conveyed by means of concrete images. The valleys of the earth as well the highest mountain peaks are his. There is nothing astonishing in the waters he produced out of the rock; the very sea was created by him. Surely he could dam it up to provide a passage for his People. And now that the procession is come to the Temple:

Come, let us adore and fall down, and weep before the God who made us.

For he is Everlasting, our God, and we are the people of his pasture and the sheep of his hand. [v. 67]

Here we witness the development of a ritual. Man, adoring God, first falls on his knees, and then puts his forehead down in the dust. This is still the practice of the monks of the East today, and the Good Friday liturgy begins in the same way. The Israelite is invited to commit himself completely to God, his creator, and to adore him, but also to keep well in mind his own peculiar vocation: he is a member of God's People and a sheep of his flock. Everlasting is his shepherd.[22]

Soon after comes the invitation to listen to the voice of the shepherd: ". . . today, may we hear his voice . . ." (v. 7). All the spiritual significance of the Feast of the Tabernacles is expressed in this verse: past events are commemorated only because of their

[22] Ps 23:1–21. Note the words: "Everlasting is my Shepherd." This theme of God the shepherd is sustained until Jesus declares that he is himself the good shepherd (Jn 10:1–21).

bearing upon today. Is this not, after all, the aim of all liturgy?

Another psalm repeats this invitation in a striking manner, a psalm that is also part of the liturgy of the Feast of the Tabernacles. We know that during this week of festivities the People lived in thatched huts. These days coincided with the full moon of the month of Tishri (September–October). Israel thus commemorated the Sinai Covenant with its gift of the Law and the sojourn in the desert. Here are some verses from this psalm (81):

Rejoice in God, our helper; sing aloud to the God of Jacob.

Take a psalm and bring hither the timbrel, the pleasant psaltery with the harp. Blow up the trumpet on the new moon, on the noted day of your solemnity. . . .

"I tried you at the waters of Meribah. Listen, O my People: I warn you! O Israel, if only you would listen to me! . . .

"But my People heard not my voice, and Israel harkened not to me. So I let them go according to the desires of their hearts: they will walk in their own conceit.

"Oh! If only my People had heard me. . . . [Ps 81:2–4, 8–9, 12–14]

The exceptional importance that tradition has attached to the episode of Meribah is evident: there it is that Israel put God to the test! The ninety-fifth psalm resumes: "Harden not your hearts as at Meribah, where your fathers tempted me in the wilderness; they tried me, and yet they had seen my works" (vv. 8–9).

They ought to have trusted him, he says, because they crossed the sea dry-shod, and he delivered them from the land of Egypt. He sweetened the waters of Mara, gave them the manna, protected them from their enemies, and made good his pledges to Abraham, Isaac, and Jacob. These are the wonders which Scripture calls "the glory of God and his signs." These signs are characteristic of God's glory, because in them we see the finger of God and a reason for trusting in him. Jesus himself will one day point out to his signs or divine works when prompting men to have faith in himself, as St. John tells us:

The works which my Father has given me to accomplish, these works that I do bear witness to me that the Father has sent me. [Jn 5:36]

If I had not done among them works such as no one else has done, they would have no sin. But now they have seen and have hated both me and the Father. . . . [Jn 15:24]

The ninety-fifth psalm ends by taking us back to the forty-year theme:

For forty years have I been despised by this generation, and I said: "A people with a perverse heart, they have not known my ways;" and I swore in my wrath: "They will never enter into my rest."

Israel's perverse heart and her lack of understanding of the ways of God constitute the whole drama of the People of God. Remembrance is made of the desert in the liturgy of the Feast of the Tabernacles in order to "call back" God's People. It is the untiring appeal of love. If no response is made to it, the day of wrath may finally arrive when the door will be forever barred to God's rest, that is, to the place where God eternally dwells. There is clearly an eschatological tone in all this. What is in question is the great rest after the combats and the wounds of the journey—the beatitude of heaven.

In their meditations the prophets take up these past events again and again in order to understand them more fully, to restate them more clearly, and through them to foretell the new wonders that God will perform. Two of them particularly deal with the mystery of the water flowing from the rock. But for these prophets the rock is above all that of Jerusalem on which the Temple rests. In the desert God announced, "I shall be before

105

you on the rock, in Horeb" (Ex 17:6), and the question the People asked was, "Is Everlasting with us, or is he not?" The rock accompanied the People, so to speak, shrouded in mystery; now Everlasting is present in the Temple erected on the rock of Jerusalem.

Read, for instance, the theological meditation of Ezechiel who, in his exile after the ruin of the first Temple, envisages the future and is taken in spirit to the land of Israel: "He brought me again to the gate of the Temple, and behold, waters issued out from under the threshold of the Temple toward the east" (Ez 47:6). In his vision the prophet sees water issuing first as a torrent and then, to emphasize its abundance, as a deep river. Wherever this water flows it brings life (even the Dead Sea is vivified); it makes fish abound and covers the earth with evergreen trees yielding new fruits every month, "because this water comes from the sanctuary."

We are dealing, therefore, with a time that is deeply eschatological, a time in which we find, as it were, a new earthly paradise thanks to this water flowing from the Temple built on the rock.

Another prophet, Zacharias, gives us a prophecy after the years of the Exile that is more characteristic still:

On the day (it will be a wondrous day which is known to Everlasting). . . . living waters will go out of Jerusalem, half of them to the east sea and half of them to the west sea, and they will be living in summer as well as in winter.

And Everlasting will be king over all the earth.

On that day Everlasting will be one and his name will be one. [Za 14:6–9]

The universal Kingdom of Everlasting is associated with this living water flowing out of Jerusalem. It is not difficult to see foreshadowed in this another water that we know very well. The prophecy ends thus:

All they that will be left of all the nations that came up against Jerusalem will go up from year to year to adore Everlasting, the king of hosts, and to keep the feast of the tabernacles. [Za 14:16]

This reminds us of the verse of the psalm in which the peaceful waters of Siloe are said to grow into a mighty river: "The stream of the river makes the city of God joyful; it sanctifies the tabernacle of the Most High" (Ps 47:5).

But like the manna, the water of the rock finds its fulfillment and the revelation of its full significance in the person of Our Lord Jesus Christ.

Consider, to begin with, the episode of the Samaritan woman. This is in the first part of the Gospel, in which the Evangelist develops the whole theme of human life. Just before this incident we hear Christ's words to Nicodemus: "Nicodemus, unless one be born again from on high of water and the Spirit, he cannot see the Kingdom of God" (Jn 3:5). And again, after the chapter on the Samaritan woman, John relates the revelation of the bread of life (Jn 6).

As Christ is sitting by the well of Jacob toward noon, a Samaritan woman comes to draw water. She does not know yet that all created things point toward a fuller life; she does not know that it is necessary to Pass-over toward the world of God under the leadership of the Messiah.

If you had known the gift of God and who it is who says to you, "Give me to drink," you would perhaps have asked him, and he would have given you a living water. [Jn 4:10]

The gift of God—as the elderly St. John relates the incident to his community at Ephesus, baptism has already been administered in the Church for well over sixty years. This means sixty years of experience in the divine life of this sacrament. The apostle does not need to explain what the gift of God means; all Christians understand this in terms of the Holy Ghost. The phrase "gift of God" is the classical reference to him. The Holy Ghost is the "gift of the Father" which Jesus has earned through his death and Resurrection. He diffuses the Spirit everywhere as a spring of living waters.

The Samaritan woman is uneasy:

Sir, you have nothing to draw with and the well is deep. Where will you get this living water? Are you greater than our father Jacob who gave us this well and drank from it himself, and his sons and his flocks? [Jn 4:11-12]

The woman hopes Christ will protest when she compares him with Jacob. She has advanced the comparison as an enormity. In reality, however, Jacob belongs to the realm of the flesh, while he who speaks to her belongs to the world of the Spirit. Christ replies:

Everyone who drinks of this water will thirst again. He, however, who drinks of the water that I will give him will never thirst.

The water that I will give him will become in him a fountain of water springing up unto life everlasting. [Jn 4:13-14]

We and this woman stand before the very Rock of Israel. Come, let us kneel and adore! Today, if we hear his voice, we must not harden our hearts as at Meribah. The woman opens her heart and the water flows in from the Rock. Immediately she herself becomes a source of water. She leaves her pitcher and speeds to the city whence she leads the Samaritans to Christ that they too may drink. "They all drank of a spiritual rock that followed them, and this rock was Christ," says St. Paul (1 Cor 10:4).

The second characteristic episode that reveals the Christ-Rock whence flow the living waters takes place in Jerusalem, appropriately enough during the Feast of the Tabernacles.

To understand fully the implication of some of St. John's words, it is necessary to recall the outline of the liturgy of this feast. It opens with some psalms: 95, which we have already commented on, and 81. One other psalm, 118, the last of the Hallel,[23] is also characteristic because of the reference this prayer of praise makes to the person of Christ. The structure of this psalm enables us to follow the processional liturgy.

At the beginning we have an invitatory:[24] Give thanks to Everlasting, for he is good; for his mercy endures forever" (Ps 118:1). This first verse develops into a short strophe in which we hear the very prayer of the Messiah. Sacred history is the history of *his* People, all encompassed within the framework of God's love:

Let Israel now say that he is good, that his mercy endures forever;

Let the house of Aaron now say that his mercy endures forever;

Let them that fear Everlasting now say that his mercy endures forever. [vv. 2–4]

The invitatory is announced by the cantor, and alternates in a lively dialogue with the response of the people.

The life of Christ is about to enter into its critical stage at the time of the Feast of the Tabernacles mentioned in the seventh chapter of St. John's Gospel. "The world hates me," Jesus says, "because I testify that their works are evil"; and again, "Why

[23] The Hallel psalms are a series (113–118) in praise of God used in the celebration of feasts. They form one of the most characteristic liturgical collections. Ps 136 is called "the great Hallel."

[24] *Invitatory* in liturgy means an invitation to prayer.

do you seek to kill me?" (Jn 7:7, 19). Now a whole sequence of verses expressive of confidence follow in Psalm 118:

I was pushed that I might fall: but Everlasting supported me.

Everlasting is my strength and my song: he has become my savior. [vv. 13-14]

The circumstances of Jesus' life are thus woven into the history of the Passover and the Exodus of his People.[25] During this feast the Israelites symbolically re-enact in Jerusalem the events of the Exodus in the desert: they live in thatched huts. The psalm mentions this fact.

The voice of rejoicing and of salvation is in the tabernacles of the just.

The right hand of Everlasting has wrought strength, the right hand of Everlasting has triumphed, the right hand of Everlasting has wrought strength. [vv. 15-16]

From verse 19 onward, we hear an echo of the procession as it enters into the Temple. Isaias called Jerusalem "the city of justice," "the faithful city," thus recalling its vocation of sanctity.[26] As the procession comes to the Temple, the people chant:

Open to me the gates of justice: I will go into them and give thanks to Everlasting. [v. 19]

To this the priests reply:

This is the gate of Everlasting: the just will enter into it. [v. 20]

[25] Moses sang the hymn of deliverance by the Red Sea: "Everlasting is my strength and my song; I owe my salvation to him" (Ex 15:2).

[26] In Is, there is a canticle that runs: "Open the gates, and let the just nation that keeps the truth enter in. . . . Hope in Everlasting forevermore, for Everlasting is the Rock" (Is 26:2-4).

The People then resume:

I will give thanks to you because you have heard me: you have become my salvation. [v. 21]

The psalm now bursts into a mysterious, oft-repeated prophecy: the prophecy of the rock discarded by the builders but finally destined to be the cornerstone.[27] This prophecy is applied to Jesus literally by St. Matthew (Mt 21:42), and is quoted again with the same reference in the Acts of the Apostles (4:11). in the Epistle to the Romans (9:33) and in several other places. This is a constantly recurring messianic tradition. We should think of this psalm as it was chanted at this particular Feast of the Tabernacles in which Jesus participated, first secretly and then openly: "The stone which the builders have rejected, the same is become the cornerstone. This is the doing of Everlasting, and it is wonderful in our eyes" (vv. 22–23).

Man's rejection of the Rock in the Passion of Jesus and God's placing it as a cornerstone in his Resurrection are now at hand. How dearly we should love to watch the face of Christ, rapt in prayer during this chant!

This extraordinary psalm continues with acclamations that will be resumed on Palm Sunday when jubilant disciples, taking up in some way the refrain of the liturgy, will strew tree branches and carry Christ in triumph into Jerusalem. During the Feast of the Tabernacles, in fact, the Jews bring fruits and branches, palms and thyrsi which they swing aloft during the chant and finally lay about the altar.

Save, Everlasting, save;[28] grant victory, Everlasting, grant victory! [v. 25]

[27] See, for example, Is 1:26, 26:2, etc.
[28] "Save can be translated with the word *Hosannah.*

111

To these acclamations the priests respond with a blessing:

Blessed be he who comes in the name of Everlasting! We have blessed you from the house of Everlasting.[29] Everlasting is God, and he has shone upon us.

Close up your ranks, branches in your hands, up to the corners of the altar. [vv. 25–27]

The last verse of the psalm repeats the opening invitation:

Give thanks to Everlasting, for he is good; for his mercy endures forever. [v. 29]

Part of the liturgy of this feast, along with the texts of Exodus on the miracle of the water sprung from the rock, is the prophecy of Zacharias about the purifying water that springs out of Jerusalem and flows into the whole world.

Each morning during this week, a procession wends its way to the fountain of Siloe at the foot of the hill on which Jerusalem is built. There a ritual pitcher made of precious metal is filled with water. On the way back to the Temple the procession chants psalms and the verse from Isaias, "You will draw water with joy at the sources of salvation" (Is 12:3). The palms, the olive branches, the greenery and fruits symbolize abundance and life bestowed by the king of creation. The climax of the procession is reached when the priests make an offering of the water before the altar.

All this enables us to recapture the atmosphere of fervor, prayer, and joy that pervades Jerusalem during this week of the Tabernacles.

Now, as St. John tells us, on the last day of the feast, the great day,[30] Jesus stands in the Temple and cries out: "If anyone

[29] The house of Everlasting is the Temple. It is from there that the priests bless the advancing procession.

[30] This great day is the evening of the last day, the seventh, or perhaps the following day, the eighth, that closed the feast.

thirst, let him come to me and drink; he who believes in me, as the Scripture says, from within him there will flow rivers of living waters" (Jn 7:37-38).

With these words, through the symbolism of the liturgy, Christ establishes a connection with the episode of the rock of the desert. This man, concrete in his individuality, Jesus of Nazareth ("What good can come out of Nazareth? Read the Scriptures and you will find that no prophet can issue out of Galilee"), the son of Mary ("We know his brothers and sisters"), he who preaches about the Kingdom of God and has healed the sick these past three years, issues an invitation: "If anyone thirst, let him come to me. . . ." To come to him means to believe in him: let him who is thirsty believe in him. He will drink abundantly and find strength and joy to march toward the Promised Land. Better still, he will become a spring himself, like the Samaritan woman.

What is this abundant water flowing from this spiritual Rock?

He said this . . . of the Spirit whom they who believed in him were to receive. . . .

Some of the crowd, therefore, when they heard these words, said, "This is truly the Prophet." [Jn 7:39-49][31]

People have been calling him the Prophet since the multiplication of the loaves; and Christ has already mentioned the necessity of believing in him.[32]

St. John is destined to watch this Rock be struck open when Christ's side is pierced while he hangs on the cross.

When Jesus dies, John says: "And bowing his head, he gave

[31] The theme of the water and the Spirit can be found all through the Bible, from the Old Testament through the baptism of Christ and into Ap 22:1-2.

[32] See pp. 107 ff.

113

up his spirit" (Jn 19:30); and then he solemnly reports an event which he has seen with his own eyes and which obviously has extraordinary importance for him:

The Jews therefore, since it was the Preparation day, in order that the bodies might not remain upon the cross on the Sabbath (for that Sabbath was a solemn day), besought Pilate that their legs might be broken and that they might be taken away.

The soldiers, therefore, came and broke the legs of the first and of the other who had been crucified with him.

But when they came to Jesus and saw that he was already dead, they did not break his legs; but one of the soldiers opened his side with a lance, *and immediately there came out blood and water.*

And he who saw it has borne witness and his witness is true, and he[33] knows that he tells the truth that you also may believe. For these things came to pass that the Scripture might be fulfilled: "Not a bone of him shall you break." And another Scripture says: "They will look upon him whom they have pierced." [Jn 19:31–37]

The Rock is now cleft. From the pierced side blood and water issue forth. Blood is a token of the sacrifice, and we shall find it again in the eucharist. Water is associated with the gift of the Spirit. The whole scene is clear before our eyes as the firm hand of St. John has drawn it for us. It is confirmed by his authentic testimony so that we may believe. We are reminded of the prophetic words of Zacharias:

I will pour upon the house of David and upon the inhabitants of Jerusalem the spirit of grace and of prayer.

And they will look upon him whom they have pierced; they will mourn for him as for an only son; and they will grieve for him as for the death of a firstborn. [Za 12:10]

[33] "He" might be John, Christ, or God.

And the prophet adds, a little further on:

On that day there will be a fountain open to the house of David and to the inhabitants of Jerusalem for the washing of sin and uncleanliness. [Za 13:1]

This is the mysterious way men are prepared for dispensations of grace. How much did the inhabitants of Jerusalem in Zacharias' time understand of all this? He spoke of a death and redemption. They perhaps desired this pure source announced by the prophet. But one day Jesus appeared, and things were far different from what people had expected; and yet faithful souls have said, as did St. John, "This, then, is what it all meant."

St. Ambrose comments:

Drink out of the twin cup of the Old and the New Testament; both contain Christ.

Slake your thirst with Christ, for he is the Rock from which water flows.

Slake your thirst with Christ, for he is the source of life.

Slake your thirst with Christ, for he is the river the waters of which gladden the City of God.

Slake your thirst with Christ, for he is peace.

Slake your thirst with Christ, for out of his bosom issue forth rivers of living water.[34]

St. John, in the Apocalypse, has the final vision of the great Feast of the Tabernacles in heaven:

After this I saw a great multitude which no man could number, out of all nations and tribes and peoples and tongues, standing before the throne and before the Lamb, clothed in white robes and with palms in their hands.

[34] St. Ambrose, *Explanatio Psalmorum*, P.L. 14:940.

And they cried with a loud voice, saying: "Salvation belongs to our God, who sits upon the throne, and to the Lamb." . . .

For the Lamb . . . will shepherd them and will guide them to the sources of living water. [Ap 7:9–10, 17]

THE PILLAR OF LIGHT

One other element in the Exodus narrative remains to be discussed, or rather to be taken up again. It is the cloud, black at first and then shining (Elohist tradition), which we should identify with the pillar of light, the column of cloud and the pillar of fire (Yahwist tradition), and finally with the "glory" spoken of in the Priestly tradition.[35]

Let us examine some of the Exodus texts.

First, Israel departs from Egypt:

And Everlasting went before them to show the way, by day in a pillar of cloud, and by night in a pillar of fire, that he might be the guide of their journey at both times.

There never failed the pillar of the cloud by day nor the pillar of fire by night, before the People. [Ex 13:21–22]

Thus says the Yahwist tradition, to emphasize that the People make their journey under God's leadership.[36] The fusion of the Yahwist and Priestly traditions—cloud and glory—is apparent in the account of the manna: "The children of Israel looked toward the wilderness, and behold; the glory of Everlasting appeared in a cloud" (Ex 16:10).

The cloud reappears on Mount Sinai at the time of the Covenant:

[35] This subject is discussed extensively and in detail by Auzou in *op. cit.*, pp. 208–215.

[36] We have already seen a second passage (Ex 14:19–20, 24). The pillar of cloud is here identified with the angel of God.

Everlasting said to Moses: "Lo! now I will come to you in the darkness of a cloud, that the People may hear me speaking to you and may believe you forever." . . .

And when the day was come and morning appeared, behold, thunders began to be heard and lightning to flash and a very thick cloud to cover the mountain, and the noise of a trumpet sounded exceeding loud, and the People that was in the camp feared. [Ex 19:9, 16]

Finally, as the Covenant is being concluded, we find Moses on the mountain, again surrounded by cloud, fire, and glory. This passage is quoted again because of the remarkable fusion of these different elements it contains:

And the glory of Everlasting dwelt upon Sinai, covering it with a cloud six days.

On the seventh day [Everlasting] called [to Moses] out of the midst of the cloud.

And the sight of the glory of Everlasting was like a burning fire upon the top of the mountain, in the eyes of the children of Israel.

And Moses, entering into the midst of the cloud, went up into the mountain; and he was there forty days and forty nights. [Ex 24:16–18]

The top of Mount Sinai is crowned with a dense cloud that is shot through with great flashes of lightning. The religious sentiment of the People leads them to see in these natural phenomena the intervention of God and his active presence—a presence woven into the concrete events of sacred history. The Hebrews see God's glory in cloud and lightning, and hear his voice in the thundering storm.

Moses climbs alone toward Everlasting. He dwells forty days and forty nights in human solitude and divine companionship. He will return to his people with the tablets of the Law.[37]

[37] See pp. 27–28.

The more familiar we are with these sacred texts, the more impressed we become with the importance of this event, for it concerns all human generations, including our own. God revealed himself in the wonders of his glory, and one man was found who could understand and respond to him. This is how we have received the Law.

Notice how Deuteronomy expresses this mystery:

And you came to the foot of the mountain, which blazed to the very sky with fire and was enveloped in a dense black cloud.

Then Everlasting spoke to you from the midst of the fire. You heard the sound of the words but saw no form. There was only a voice. And [Everlasting] proclaimed to you his Covenant, which he commanded you to keep: the Ten Commandments, which he wrote on two tablets of stone. [Dt 4:11–13]

Cloud and glory are specially present in the place where God resides. The two dwellings of God in the Old Testament are looked upon by sacred history as related to each other: the mystery of the Temple of Jerusalem has sprung up from the remembrance of the Meeting Tent of the desert.

The cloud covered the Meeting Tent,[38] and the glory of Everlasting filled it. Neither could Moses go into the Tent, the cloud covering all things and the majesty of Everlasting shining, for the cloud had covered all.

If at any time the cloud left the Tent, the children of Israel went forward on their journey. If it did not, they remained where they were.

For the cloud of Everlasting hung over the Tent by day and the fire by night in the sight of all the children of Israel.

Thus it was in all the stages of their journey. [Ex 40:32–36]

[38] See pp. 33 ff.

This is indeed a picture of God-with-us.

When David, the generous and warm-hearted king, thinks of building a Temple to Everlasting, God's first response is this:

I have not dwelt in a house from the day that I brought the children of Israel out of the land of Egypt even to this day, but I was in their camp, under a Tent, in all the time that I have journeyed with the children of Israel. . . . [2 S 7:6–7]

However, since the People of God are now settled in the Land of Promise, God finally gives his consent, and Solomon is allowed to build the Temple.

When it is time for the consecration of the Temple, the priests transfer the Ark of the Covenant from the Tent where it rests to the Holy of Holies, the hidden and sacred dwelling place built to house it.

And it came to pass, when the priests came out of the sanctuary, that a cloud filled the house of Everlasting, and the priests could not stand to minister because of the cloud; for the glory of Everlasting had filled the house. [1 K 8:10–11]

If we turn to the Virgin Mary at Nazareth when the angel makes his great announcement, "Hail, full of grace, the Lord is with thee," we see her become the "throne [of Wisdom] in a pillar of cloud" (Sir 24:7). In her the Word of God becomes fully and forever Emmanuel—God-with-us—and she herself the glory-filled Temple of Everlasting. How can that be, she asks? To her question, the angel replies: "The Holy Spirit will come upon you, and the power of the Most High will take you under his shadow" (Lk 1:35).

The cloud has become a shadow, but both are symbols of the same presence and the same activity.

And thus we come to Jesus himself. In his Prologue, John says,

"And the Word was made flesh, and pitched his tent among us,[39] and we saw his glory . . ." (Jn 1:14). Truly, he is the brightness of his Father's glory (Heb. 1:3), in him dwells bodily the fullness of the Godhead (Col 2:9).

To return to the Feast of the Tabernacles, we have already mentioned its great sign of the water flowing out of the rock. There is another important element in its ritual. After the celebration of the water comes the celebration of the light: the Temple is illuminated with immense candelabra which are placed in the women's enclosure and keep burning throughout the night. Viewed from the Mount of Olives which is opposite Jerusalem, the sight is gorgeous. It looks as if the Temple were the great pillar of light in the desert of the world. Some Levites, standing on the steps which lead from the women's enclosure to the place reserved for men, are chanting psalms.

This part of the feast lends to all Jerusalem an atmosphere of exceptional prayerfulness and religious jubilation.

St. John observes (Jn 8:20) that Jesus is standing by the treasury, that is, near the boxes destined to receive the offerings and thus in the midst of the burning candelabra, when he says: "I am the light of the world. He who follows me will not walk in darkness but will have the light of life" (Jn 8:12).

The episodes of the Exodus lend significance to this proclamation, "I am the light!" The texts on the Exodus from Egypt are read out during this feast. He who follows Jesus, as the Hebrews have followed the pillar of light in the desert, march on toward the Land of Promise.

Light and life go together in this eastern land. When Jesus

[39] This, then, is what the humble Tent of the desert was preparing us for!

illustrates the meaning of his assertion by restoring the sight of the man born blind (Jn 9), he performs a sign almost as astonishing as when he restores life to Lazarus four days after his death.[40]

Light and life! When Jesus speaks thus, the prophecy of Isaias which we recite on Christmas night finds its fulfillment: "The people that walked in darkness have seen a great light; to them that dwelt in the region of the shadow of death a light has appeared" (Is 9:2). So does another prophecy, among the most wonderful in Third Isaias, where the prophet, after his return from exile, foresees Jerusalem become beautifully resplendent because the glory of Everlasting, Jesus, has appeared in her midst:

Arise, be enlightened, O Jerusalem, for your light is come and the glory of Everlasting is risen upon you. For behold, darkness will cover the earth, and a mist the people; but over you arises Everlasting, and his glory appears. . . .

And the Gentiles walk toward your light and kings toward your rising brightness. [Is 60:1–3]

Such is the revelation of the Christ-Light in the context of the Feast of the Tabernacles.

To round out the subject of cloud, glory, and pillar of light, we should take up again the account of the Transfiguration[41] with its evocation of the Tents, the glory of Jesus, the discourse on his Passover, and the cloud that covers the mountain. We should also recall the cloud that steals Jesus from the gaze of his apostles on his Ascension, and finally his last return and judgment.

And then they will see the Son of man coming upon the clouds with great power and majesty; and then he will send forth his angels and

---

[40] "Could not he who opened the eyes of the blind have caused that this man should not die" (Jn 11:37).

[41] Lk 9:28–36; see pp. 53–58.

will gather his elect from the four winds, from the uttermost parts of the earth to the uttermost parts of heaven. [Mk 13:26–27]

These are some of the thoughts suggested by the forty years of the People of God in the desert—forty years of chastisement and tribulation, but also forty years of grace, forty years of training in the Covenant and of preparation for the Promised Land.

The Great Fast of Jesus Christ

And after fasting forty days and forty nights, [Jesus] was hungry.
[Mt 4:2]

CROSSING THE JORDAN

". . . all [our fathers] were baptized in Moses, in the cloud and
in the sea." We have endeavored to show what meaning Paul
gives to this passage through the Sea of Reeds in his first Epistle
to the Corinthians (10:2).

This "baptism" launched the People of God upon their Exodus
through the desert. But this period of sacred history, so rich in
divine interventions, in gifts and institutions, these forty years
that have molded God's People ("I will be their God and they
will be my People") terminate as they have begun—with a
similar sign. We refer to the crossing of the Jordan.

At the start, pursued by the Egyptians, the children of Israel
cross the Red Sea under the leadership of Moses. At the end, to
leave the desert behind and enter the Promised Land, they cross
the Jordan under the leadership of Josue.[1] The whole of the
Exodus is thus placed between this double sign of water.

First, Josue directs the People to sanctify themselves: "Sanctify
yourselves, for tomorrow Everlasting will do wonders among
you" (Jos 3:5). To sanctify oneself means to dispose oneself to
the operation of the holy grace of God. Before Everlasting's great
manifestation on Sinai, Moses commands the People to sanctify
themselves in two ways: first, by washing their garments, a rite

---

[1] The account of the crossing of the Jordan obviously belongs to the
same literary genre as that of the passage through the Red Sea.

that speaks for itself—it fosters a definite orientation of the soul; and second, by abstaining temporarily from sexual intercourse (Ex 19:10–15). This, too, is very appropriate. Sexual relations are absorbing and earth-binding, while this is a time to prepare oneself to rise to God. This ascent cannot be effected without renunciation and abstinence in favor of spiritual freedom and supernatural mysteries. This will be Paul's argument in favor of virginity.[2]

Next, the account of Josue places this leader in the immediate wake of Moses himself:

Everlasting said to Josue: "This day will I begin to exalt you before Israel, that they may know that as I was with Moses, so I will be with you also.

"And command the priests that carry the Ark of the Covenant, and say to them: 'When you will have entered into part of the water of the Jordan, remain there.' " [Jos. 3:7–8]

In a sense, the baptism in the Red Sea terminates with the Baptism in the Jordan. "From this sign you will know that a living God is in your midst," adds Josue (3:10).

The sign is part of the epic atmosphere that pervades this narrative, similar to that at the beginning of Exodus. The present text shows an even more pedagogical and spiritual composition than the account in Exodus; it is more stylized and less concrete, more solemn and less spontaneous, but it conveys an identical message:

---

[2] "He who is unmarried is concerned about the things of the Lord, how he may please God, whereas he who is married is concerned about the things of the world, how he may please his wife [though this may be his duty]; and he is divided" (1 Cor 7:32–33). This is not to discredit marriage but to state a principle which, applied practically and generously, defines different vocations. If we are sincere and honest, we must admit that virginity brings with it a special orientation toward the Kingdom of God.

So the People went out of their tents to cross the Jordan; and the priests that carried the Ark of the Covenant went on before them.

And as soon as they came into the Jordan and their feet were dipped in part of the water (now the Jordan, it being harvest time, had filled its banks), the waters that came down from above stood in one place and swelled up like a mountain, and were seen afar off from the city that is called Adom to the place of Sarthan; but those that were beneath ran down to the Sea of Araba (which is now called the Dead Sea) until they completely failed.[3] And the People marched over against Jericho. The priests that carried the Ark of the Covenant of Everlasting stood firm upon dry ground in the midst of the Jordan until all the People crossed the river that was dried up. . . .

And the People made haste and crossed over. . . .[4]

And when they that carried the Ark of the Covenant of Everlasting were come to the other bank and began to tread on dry ground, the waters returned to the river and ran as they were wont before. [Jos 3:14–17, 4:10, 18]

CHRIST'S BAPTISM

Jesus begins his public life in the waters of the Jordan, not far from Jericho, and terminates his exodus with the celebration of the Passover: ". . . hour had come for him to pass from this world to the Father" (Jn 13:1).

The last remnant of his People, he re-enacts all their history, and the three years of his public ministry correspond to Israel's forty years in the desert—a period also rich in manifestations, institutions, and miracles.

Just at this time John the Baptist is preaching penance in the

[3] The Bible of Jerusalem relates the statement of an Arabian historian. In 1267 the Jordan ceased to flow for six hours when some underground upheavals had obstructed the valley, precisely in this region of Adamma-Damich.

[4] This haste reminds us of the haste of the first Passover (Ex 12:11).

Judaean desert; but taking up the joyful prophecy of the end of the Babylonian Exile, he says he is "the voice of one crying in the wilderness: 'Prepare the way of Everlasting; make straight in the wilderness the paths of our God'" (Is 40:3). And the people gathered round him, hearing his words, wonder whether a new exodus, a new "betrothal of the desert" (Jer 2:2), is about to begin again. "And they, confessing their sins, were baptized by him in the Jordan" (Mt 3:6).

It is here that Jesus makes his appearance:

Then Jesus came from Galilee to John to be baptized by him. And John was for hindering him, and said: "It is I who ought to be baptized by you, and do you come to me?"

But Jesus answered and said to him: "Let it be so now, for so it becomes us to fulfill all justice." Then he permitted him. [Mt 3:13–15]

Jesus comes *in order* to be baptized. When John declines Jesus insists, just as he will insist, in spite of Peter's protests at the last supper, on washing the disciples' feet. Who can fathom God's designs? We often come across incomprehensible events willed by God and laden with inscrutable significance. It is through such events that all justice is to be fulfilled—that the holiness prepared and announced in the Old Testament is to attain to its full realization.

When Christ descends into the waters of the Jordan, a stupendous manifestation takes place; the veil is lifted for a moment from the secret of God:

And when Jesus had been baptized, he immediately came up from the water, and behold, the heavens were opened to him, and [John] saw the Spirit of God descending as a dove and coming upon [Jesus].

And behold, a voice from the heavens said: "This is my beloved Son,[5] in whom I am well pleased." [Mt 3:16-17]

Let us pause here for a moment to contemplate the scene. Let us listen attentively to these words of the Father. Religion is not only morality—doing good and avoiding evil—nor mere philanthropy, that is, a sentiment of pity or compassion for our brethren. The Christian religion is above all a revelation of God in Christ. This is the basis for an intimate familiarity, a friendship with God.

The Father manifests himself to man because he loves him, because man is truly his child: "No longer do I call you servants, because the servant does not know what his master does; but I have called you friends, because all things that I have heard from my Father I have made known to you" (Jn 15:15).

The Voice of the Father

The heavens open just as Christ gains the river bank again, "while in prayer," adds St. Luke (3:21). A voice is heard from above—the voice of the Father. The Father is invisible; no one has ever seen him, and no one can ever see him without dying. Only Christ, in heaven, will introduce us to the vision of him (1 Cor 13:12).

But how full our perception is from hearing the voice by the Jordan! The voice reveals the joy of the Father: "my Son," he says as he introduces Jesus to us; "my beloved Son, in whom I am well pleased."

In what does this pleasure of the Father consist? It consists in the gift he makes of his beloved Son, standing there in the water of the Jordan, in the midst of sinners.

[5] Lk 3:22 and Mk 1:11 tell us that the voice of the Father is addressed directly to Jesus: "You are my beloved Son . . . ." We give here a rendering that differs somewhat from the Bible of Jerusalem.

It is God's love that is being revealed to us here. God loves to love; his pleasure is in the salvation of man:

For God so loved the world that he gave his only-begotten Son. . . .

For God did not send his Son into the world in order to judge the world, but that the world might be saved through him. [Jn 3:16–17]

The Mystery of Christ

The voice of the Father sanctions, in advance, the whole life of Jesus Christ. "Men, do not be astonished," it seems to say, "by what my Son will do, but listen to him. In him I have placed all my joy. All his actions, all his words, his whole life will manifest my love."

"What is visible of the invisible Father is Christ; what of the visible Christ is invisible is the Father," says St. Irenaeus.[6]

Christ is the Father's envoy.[7]

But from the very beginning he is also pointed out as the mysterious suffering servant mentioned in the four poems of the servant in Isaias' Book of Consolation. At the very beginning of the first poem, the Father's voice reveals the Consecration of the servant. "Behold my servant: I will uphold him, my elect in whom my soul delights. I have placed my spirit upon him that he may bring judgment to the nations" (Is 42:1). For servant, the Septuagint uses the Greek word *pais,* which has a shade of meaning suggesting *child*—my child—or my *family servant.*

Over this Servant God spreads his spirit, and to him he entrusts the mission of conveying to the nations (that is, the heathens) judgment, or justice, or better still sanctity.[8] In the

---

[6] *Adversus Haereses,* IV, 6, 3.

[7] E.g., Jn 8:16, and several other passages.

[8] This passage of Isaias is quoted twice more by St. Matthew (12:18 and 17:5), who obviously thinks it very important.

context of this great and mysterious prophecy is Christ introduced by the Father on the banks of the Jordan.

One day Paul will meditate and comment on this servant in one of the most triumphant hymns of the New Testament:

Have within you the same sentiments that were also in Jesus Christ, who, though in the "form" of God, did not consider being equal to God a thing to be clung to, but effaced himself, taking the form of a servant.

Become similar to men and appearing in the form of men, he humbled himself, becoming obedient to death, even the death of the cross.

Therefore, God also has exalted him and has bestowed on him a name that is above all names, so that at the name of Jesus every knee should bend, of those in heaven, on earth, and under the earth, and every tongue should confess that the Lord Jesus Christ is in the glory of God the Father. [Phil 2:5–11][9]

Servant and Lord, in the glory of God the Father—this is how Jesus appears from the very first moment of his public life, at his baptism in the Jordan.

There is yet one more Person who appears at this manifestation. Jesus descends into the river and humbles himself; the waters cover him. This symbolizes death. Then he climbs back to the bank, the heavens open, the Father's voice is heard, and the Spirit descends upon him.

The Descent of the Spirit

Water and Spirit—Christ will soon wed the two in his words to Nicodemus: "Unless a man be born again of water and the Spirit, he cannot enter into the Kingdom of God" (Jn 3:5).[10]

[9] From the French translation of Msgr. Cerfaux, *Recueil Cerfaux,* II, 426.
[10] See p. 34.

Spirit or breath—the Hebrew has the same word for both.

Genesis speaks of the Spirit of God, hovering over the primordial waters as soon as a creation appears that is capable of grace (Gn 1:2).

The breath of God passes over the waters of the Deluge to allow the earth to begin anew (Gn 8:21).

It is with his mighty breath that Everlasting carves a passage for his People through the Sea of Reeds (Ex 14:21).

The Spirit descends now upon Jesus in the River Jordan, but not for a brief moment or in a fleeting contact—he remains. John the Baptist bears witness to it in simple words, and we are told of this great discovery of his. Jesus is his cousin; nevertheless, up to this baptism John has not really known him. It takes the sign of the indwelling Spirit for him to recognize in Jesus of Nazareth the Elect of God, that is, this mysterious servant mentioned in Isaias (42:1), the Lamb of God.[11] It is to reveal him to the world that the Baptist, without being aware of his role, has come to the Jordan.

The next day John saw Jesus coming to him, and he said: "Behold the Lamb of God, who takes away the sins of the world! This is he of whom I said: 'After me there comes one who has been set above me because he was before me.'

"And I did not know him. But that he may be known to Israel, therefore have I come baptizing with water."

And John bore witness, saying: "I beheld the Spirit descending as a dove from heaven, and it abode upon him. And I did not know him. But he who sent me to baptize with water said to me: 'He upon whom you will see the Spirit descending and abiding upon him, he it is who baptizes with the Holy Spirit.'

"And I have seen and have borne witness that this is the Elect of God." [Jn 1:29–34]

[11] Is 53, the fourth and greatest poem of the servant (v. 7).

130

He on whom the Spirit will rest, he it is who baptizes in the Holy Ghost!

In the Matins of Epiphany in Byzantine sacred liturgy, there is a characteristic passage that shows us how the Church understands and honors the baptism of Christ:

Today heaven and earth rejoice, watching the Lord being baptized and drowning in the water the great load of our sins.

The human soul is illuminated because, delivered from the shadow of sin, she puts on a divine and incorruptible garment.

The Kingdom of God is at hand. Christ, announced by the Law and the prophets, comes to regenerate us in his divine baptism.

You are a mighty torrent, you who have created the sea and the water springs; you come to these waters to wash us yourself, who are to everyone cleanliness and purification.

You are a gulf of truth, O Christ!

You, the undefiled water source! How could the Jordan hold you?

You are the sun that knows no twilight!

You have illuminated your sacred flesh as a torch in the midst of the Jordan.

You have found man's image soiled with passion and sin, and have washed it through your baptism!

THE FORTY DAYS IN THE DESERT

From the baptism of Christ, we pass immediately to his retreat in the desert. The two events go together.

The Holy Spirit has descended upon Christ, and he now leads Christ into solitude to engage in a combat with the tempter. With this conflict the Messiah commences his public life.

Then Jesus was led into the desert by the Spirit to be tempted by the devil.

131

And after fasting forty days and forty nights, he was hungry. And the Tempter came to him and said ... [Mt 4:1–2]

To understand the full meaning of this scene, we must consider its several biblical elements: the desert itself, Christ's fasting and prayer, and the three temptations.

The Desert

We have already visited the desert on several occasions in the course of this book. Here Moses and Elias spent their apprenticeships for their individual vocations, as law-giver and prophet respectively; here they both regenerated their souls in long penitential retreats.

God's People were tested and forged in the desert for forty years.

When the prophets envisaged a new Covenant, they associated it with the desert: "I ... will lead her into the wilderness" (Hos 2:14)—a promise of Everlasting!

In the Old Testament, the desert represents the sacred place where God can be found. At the same time, it is the place of temptation.

And now, Christ too comes to the desert.

According to the tradition, the scene of Christ's temptation is Djebel Karantal, bare and forbidding, that lifts its massive heights around the plains of Jericho, a good two hours' walk from the scene of Christ's baptism. Today a monastery nestles halfway up the side of this mountain, and several caves yawn in its rocky walls.

Coming to this desert, Christ not only represents God's People by re-enacting their history but, after the manifestation in the Jordan, he appears more appropriately still as a new Adam, the

132

Man made after the image of God, the Son of God. He comes to train in the life of the desert before introducing all creation into the paradise of God, his Father. Thus he finds in it temptation and the tempter himself.

How good it would be if everything were harmonious and peaceful, natural and guileless; but no; the world is chaotic and disorderly, full of hate and devastated by death. There exists a personal being, an enemy of God. We meet him everywhere, from Genesis right up through the Apocalypse.

To understand something of the antagonism that exists between Christ and the devil, we must understand the Gospel statement that Jesus is truth (Jn 14:15). "This is why I have come into the world, to bear witness to the truth. Everyone who is of the truth hears my voice" (Jn 18:37).

In the desert where he now is, Christ adores the Father in spirit and truth (Jn 4:23); and as he does so, in comes the devil whom Jesus will call with loathing "the liar, the father of lies" (Jn 14:5). Hence no compromise is possible: their respective attitudes toward truth are diametrically opposed.

Jesus is life (Jn 4:10). His whole mission is to bring life.

. . . he who hears my word . . . has passed from death to life. . . .

For as the Father has life in himself, even so he has given to the Son also to have life in himself. [Jn 5:24, 26]

He reveals the living water to the Samaritan woman and the bread of life to his disciples:

I am the living bread that has come down from heaven. If anyone eat of this bread, he will live forever. . . .

As the living Father has sent me, and as I live because of the Father, so he who eats me, he also will live because of me. [Jn 6:51, 58]

133

He who now prowls in the desert and approaches Jesus, Christ will also call "a murderer from the beginning" (Jn 8:44). What a clash is about to take place! It will end only on the cross with Jesus' death (a death, however, voluntary and freely accepted—"No one takes [my life] from me, but I lay it down of myself" (Jn 10:18) and with the final downfall of the enemy. The Easter sequence reads, "Death and Life for mastery did fight a wondrous duel; the King of Life laid down his life but rose and reigns alive."

Jesus comes to seek men's hearts: "If anyone love me, he will keep my word, and my Father will love him; and we will come to him and make our abode with him" (Jn 14:23).

The devil is Christ's rival. He it is who contends against Christ for man's soul. The Evangelist points out a tragic detail in this conflict: Judas, at the last supper, accepts the dipped bit of bread from the hand of Jesus, "And after the morsel, Satan entered into him. And Jesus said to him: 'What you do, do quickly'" (Jn 13:27).

Finally, the Kingdom that Jesus comes to inaugurate is not of this world. The reason Christ is in the desert is to prepare himself for the announcement of this Kingdom—how we may enter it (by water and the Holy Ghost), what its charter is (the beatitudes), what its foundation is, and how the gates of hell will not prevail against it.

The prince of this world whom Jesus will overthrow[12] is just now advancing toward him.

What will be Christ's weapons in the conflict? What will he do during his sojourn in the desert, this preparation for his public ministry?

---

[12] ". . . now will the prince of this world be cast out. And I, . . . lifted up from the earth, will draw all things to myself" (Jn 12:31–32).

Fasting and Prayer

It is from personal experience that Christ will assure his disciples that one kind of demon cannot be overcome except through fasting and prayer (Mk 9:25). And in the Garden of Olives he will say: "Watch and pray, lest you fall into temptation. The spirit indeed is willing, but the flesh is weak" (Mt 26:41). The apostles are so weak! He himself has clashed with the enemy, and he knows him well.

Fasting is a traditional spiritual discipline. We need only think of Moses' great periods of fasting on Sinai. Reduction of bodily food is a means to an abundance of divine nourishment. Fasting is a prayer of the body that acknowledges its utter dependence on God. To us Christians, fasting has no value except in relation to faith. The Church will never cease contemplating Christ fasting. All arguments advanced by human interests against fasting fall to the ground before this evangelical picture of a fasting Christ.

Jesus refrains from tasting bread—but he feeds on the word of God. It is interesting to observe how he reacts to temptation. He opposes the word of God to the devil, saying, "It is written!" He appeals to Scripture, and in a special manner to Deuteronomy, that book so replete with prophetic inspiration, quoting three passages from it that are very close to one another.[13] Christ seems to be thinking about these chapters, to be meditating on them in his Father's presence when the demon crawls by to tempt him.

This is the scene portrayed by the Gospel, a scene laden with deep significance.

It should remind us of Christ's intimate union with the Father, of which we have had a glimpse in the manifestation of the Jordan: "This is my beloved Son, in whom I am well pleased."

[13] Dt 6:13, 16; 8:3.

This love of the Father, deep down in the human heart of Christ, pervades the forty days and forty nights.

Face to face with Jesus, the devil is perturbed: this man intrigues him. In him the devil senses the conqueror, without being quite sure of it. This suspicion is to last all through the public life of Christ: "If you are the Son of God. . . ." We know who you are . . ." shout those possessed by Satan. We see in this the reaction of a creature—even a spiritual creature—to the mystery of the Word made flesh.

The First Temptation

At the end of the long fast, the Son of Man is hungry, just as he will one day be thirsty, feel the need of sleep, and experience sorrow.[14]

It is a man, therefore, that the devil approaches, in the same crafty way as he approached our first parents in the earthly paradise and asked, "Why has God forbidden you the fruits of all the trees of the garden?" (Gn 3:1).

And the tempter came and said to him: "If you are the Son of God, command that these stones become loaves of bread." [Mt 4:3]

What actually is Satan's suggestion? He suggests that Christ use the power to work miracles and signs given him to announce the Kingdom of God for a temporal and personal advantage. "Help yourself," he seems to say; "use your powers for your own profit."

What a bad start that would be for Christ's mission! The suggestion at first might appear a slight abuse of power, almost a legitimate one. And yet, had Christ consented, what would be

[14] See Jn 4:7 and 19:28; Mk 4:38; and Heb 5:7–9.

really left of the Savior and his holiness? We would have not the Kingdom of God but rather a kingdom of Arabian nights! Everything would be ruined.

This could never be. Listen to Jesus' answer. It betrays no interior conflicts; it is calm, serene, lucid.

It is written: "Not by bread alone does a man live but by every word that comes from the mouth of God."[15]

Christ's temptation is real, as real as that of his People in the desert when their provisions were exhausted and their hearts turned again to the flesh pots of Egypt. But Christ wants to teach us the need we have to be fed by God, to depend on him. Christ here lives out the mystery of the manna before he explains it to his disciples.

The Second Temptation

Then the devil took him into the Holy City and set him on the pinnacle of the Temple, and said to him:
"If you are the Son of God, throw yourself down, for it is written: 'He will give his angels charge over you, and upon their hands they will carry you, lest you dash your foot against a stone.' "[16]

We observe the technique used by the devil to tempt this man fasting in the desert. He "took him" (in imagination? by suggestion?). Isn't this the technique he uses with us, too? And where does he carry Jesus? To the Holy City. Religion comes in here. The devil places Christ on the pinnacle of the Temple. We know this intersection of the two walls of the Temple, looking precipitously over the Cedron and the Tyropheon valleys.

"If you are . . ." Who is this man, in fact? During the public

[15] Mt 4:4; Christ is quoting from Dt 8:3.
[16] Mt 4:5–6; the devil is quoting Ps 91:11–12.

life of Jesus, this becomes more and more intriguing to those around him as time goes on. Christ himself will pose the question to his apostles just before the first foretelling of his passover: "What do men say that the Son of man is? . . . But who do you say that I am?" (Mt 16:13, 16).

The devil makes use of the very words of God.

There is no automatism in religion, or in Scripture, or in the sacraments. Scripture brings life only through the Holy Spirit. It can also serve to poison, to kill. One can use it as a tool, bend it to one's own will instead of allowing oneself to be molded by it.

The devil quotes Psalm 91, which describes life in the desert. Jesus may be praying this very psalm at Djebel Karantal. It is a prayer of abandonment of self to God's will, a prayer that breathes forth confidence and peace.

What specifically does this second temptation consist of? It consists of the challenging demand that God manifest himself to us by the signs *we* prescribe. It consists of tempting God, putting God to the test—precisely as the People did at Massah and Meribah: "Is Everlasting with us, or is he not?" (Ex 17:7). For Christ, it concerns the means to be used in his messianic mission, and will recur in the Gospel:

Then certain of the Scribes and Pharisees answered him, saying: "Master, we would like to see a sign from you."

He answered and said to them: "An evil and adulterous generation demands a sign, and no sign will be given it but the sign of Jonas the prophet.

"For even as Jonas was in the belly of the fish three days and three nights, so will the Son of man be three days and three nights in the heart of the earth." [Mt 12:38-40]

When we demand that God show himself as we dictate, we exhibit our lack of confidence and prevent him from coming to us

138

in *his own way*—in the strength of Christ's weakness, in the mystery of his conflict, his death, his Resurrection.[17]

Were Jesus, on the pinnacle of the Temple, to lose for one instant his self-mastery, were he to allow himself the least giddiness, were he to choose to throw himself down and appear as descended from heaven into the very heart of the religious life of his People, were he to choose to be an earthly Messiah, the Messiah of a frenzied populace—there would no longer be a divine mystery or a religious faith. He might arouse admiration and astonishment among the milling crowd, but only as a kind of trickster. "For false christs and false prophets will arise, and will show great signs and wonders, so as to lead astray, if possible, even the elect" (Mt 24:24).

Christ's answer to Satan is perfectly simple, religious, and final, a commandment of God:

It is again written: "You shall not tempt the Lord your God." [Mt 4:7]

These last words are from Deuteronomy. In them the prophetic tradition has embodied the remembrance of Massah and Meribah, keeping the lesson of the desert alive.

It is quite clear that no one could be farther removed from the spirit of Christ, so calm, spiritual, reserved, ever led by the Spirit of God, than the man who allows himself to become the tool of the spirit of evil. The Antichrist who is to appear at the end of the world, a creature given over to the power of Satan, is thus described by St. Paul:

17 To the angel who announces to him the happy news that he will become a father, Zacharias replies with a troubled question: couldn't the angel give him a sign? And he gets his sign: he becomes dumb on the spot (Lk 1:18-20). Peter will rebel against the prospect of Christ's Passion, and Jesus will call him "Satan!" (Mt 16:23). The passers-by and the high priests will tempt Christ on the cross: let him give them a sign—let him come down from the cross, and they will believe in him (Mt 27:39-44).

... first[18] ... the man of sin [must be] revealed, the son of perdition, the adversary,[19] who exalts himself above all that is called God, or that is worshiped, so that he sits in the Temple of God and gives himself out as if he were God. ...

His coming is according to the working of Satan, with all power and signs and lying wonders and with all wicked deception to all those who are perishing. For they have not accepted the love of truth that might have saved them. [2 Th 3–4, 9–10]

The Antichrist wields a considerable power, communicated to him by the devil. He raises himself up to God's place and works signs and wonders. But let no one fear even this mighty rebel, for his power will be short-lived. He will not be able to harm the little ones, the humble, the redeemed, those who possess the love of truth. No sooner will the impious one reveal himself fully than "the Lord Jesus Christ will slay [him] with the breath of his mouth and will destroy [him] with the brightness of his coming" (2 Th 2:8).

When Christ appears in his glory, nothing more will be heard of the Antichrist, and the devil will be made permanently powerless. In a cry of joy, uttered under the impulse of the Holy Spirit, Jesus will one day tell his disciples, "I watched Satan falling like lightning from heaven" (Lk 10:18).

The Third Temptation

The third temptation is still more important, since it concerns the transcendent sovereignty of God and the adoration due him. The People experienced this awful temptation in the desert when they made to themselves a golden calf.

[18] That is, before the glorious second coming of Christ and our reunion with him.

[19] The Antichrist is here described as the man of sin, the lost being destined to perdition (in contrast to those who are saved)—in short, Jesus' adversary.

Here, finally, the demon casts off his mask and stakes his all. Nothing remains on the scene now except these two masters and their two kingdoms. Satan cannot remain concealed much longer under the disguise of an angel of light.

Again, the devil took him to a very high mountain, and showed him all the kingdoms of the world and the glory of them.

And he said to him: "All these things will I give you if you will fall down and worship me." [Mt 4:8–9]

The devil again "takes" Jesus, and once more, in spirit, Christ surveys for a moment all the kingdoms of the earth.

Jesus knows the beauty of creation and loves men. He is king, and comes to announce the Kingdom of heaven. But since the first sin there has been an ambiguity in the term *world*. *World* may signify God's creation, made by him and dressed in his splendor, "the fringe of God's garment." In this sense, "[The Word] was in the world, and the world was made through him . . ." (Jn 1:10). But the same term may mean, too, the world ruined by sin, the world become God's enemy, a world of which Satan is king. It is perfectly true that the devil wields a certain power over and reigns in the world. In the Gospel of St. Luke, he says:

To you will I give all this power and all this glory; for to me they have been delivered and to whomsoever I will give them.

Therefore, if you will worship me, the whole will be yours. [Lk 4:6–7]

In the Apocalypse of St. John, we are told how the demon transfers his power to the beast (which, here, stands for the Roman Empire): "The dragon gave to the beast his own might and great authority with an immense empire" (Ap 13:2). Our theology has left off thinking in such terms, but we cannot ignore them just because they embarrass us; they are eminently biblical. A mystery of evil exists that cannot be solved except in relation to this empire of Satan; nor can the dramatic course of Christ's life.

About to begin his passion, Christ says: "Now is the Judgment of the world; now will the prince of this world be cast out. And I, if I be lifted up from the earth, will draw all things to myself" (Jn 12:31–32).

The conflict comes to a climax here. The mystery of Satan consists in the negation of the light of the cross. This truth must never be forgotten!

This is the meaning of the third temptation at the commencement of Christ's public life. The devil throws down his mask in the desert before this man who fasts and prays. This is a fight to the finish. We can almost hear the emphatic words of the discourse after the Last Supper:

I will no longer speak much with you, for the prince of this world is coming, and in me he has nothing.

But he comes that the world may know that I love the Father and that I do as the Father has commanded me. [Jn 14:30–31]

". . . that the world may know that I love the Father"—this is the truth that lights up the desert!

Then Jesus said: "Begone, Satan! For it is written: 'The Lord your God shall you worship, and him only shall you serve.' " [Mt 4:10]

And that is final. Those are the terms laid down by the conqueror.[20] For the third time Christ vanquishes the devil with the word of God (Dt 6:13). Truly, "loyalty is an armor and a shield" (Ps 90:4).

[20] The same words will be addressed again to the devil when he makes use of Peter's human views to oppose the mystery of the passion of Christ: "Begone, Satan! You are a scandal to me!" (Mt 16:23).

Then the devil left him, and behold, angels came and ministered to him. [Mt 4:11]

Christ's retirement in the desert is over. Temptation is overcome, and Jesus can now announce the Kingdom of heaven, for he *is* the Lord of heaven, of the Kingdom which none may enter unless he be born again from on high of water and the Holy Spirit (Jn 3:3–5).

Now that the devil has left him, angels appear. They, too, are revealed in the Gospel, having first been introduced in the Old Testament. They, too, are objects of the faith of the Church, a faith founded on Scripture and expressed by the liturgy.

"And behold, angels came and ministered to him" (Mt 4:11). These divine messengers accompany Christ all through his earthly life. Gabriel announces to Mary the Incarnation of the Word (Lk 1:26–38). Angels give the glad tidings to the shepherds of Bethlehem (Lk 1:9–14). A heavenly messenger warns Joseph to fly to Egypt, and later tells him he may return home (Mt 2:13–19). An angel consoles the man Jesus in his agony (Lk 22:43). Angels proclaim the Easter message (Mt 28:2–7, Mk 16:5–7, Lk 24:4). Finally, after Christ's Ascension, angels launch the apostles on their mission and focus the Church's gaze toward the whole world as well as toward the final coming of Jesus (Acts 1:9–11).

Angels, then, appear in the desert and minister to Christ. And later, Jesus says, "If I cast out devils by the Spirit of God, then the Kingdom of God has come upon you" (Mt 12:28).

Finally, when the Kingdom of heaven is established in its glorious plenitude, when Christ reveals himself in his final advent, he will once more be escorted by all his holy angels:

And then they will see the Son of man coming upon the clouds with great power and majesty; and then he will send forth his angels and will gather his elect from the four winds, from the uttermost parts of the earth to the uttermost parts of heaven. [Mk 13:26–27]

Thus, Jesus' retreat in the Judaean desert takes place against a sublime and mysterious eschatological background.

The messianic mission of Christ, consecrated God's servant in the baptism in the Jordan, the temptations and filial loyalty of Christ in the desert, the bitterness of the conflict and the joyful advent of salvation are the essential features of these forty days of preparation in the wilderness for the Father's envoy to the world.

The Forty Days of Fulfillment

. . . during forty days [Jesus] appeared to them and spoke of the Kingdom of God. [Acts 1:3]

CHRIST's public life begins with the forty days in the desert of Djebel Karantal. There, after his Baptism, he relives the Exodus of his People.

At the end of his earthly mission, between his deliverance of the souls in Hades[1] and his final entry into the true Promised Land, Jesus spends one last period of forty days.

COMPARISONS OF THE TWO FORTY-DAY PERIODS

When we study the two forty-day periods in Christ's time on earth, we are immediately struck by the contrasts between them.

Christ's Presence

At Djebel Karantal, Jesus appears as our brother, surrounded by a sinning world and subject to the devil's temptations.

In this other period of forty days, we witness a different type of presence: that of the risen Christ. He appears "in another shape" (Mk 16:12). At first, he is not recognized. Magdalene mistakes him for a gardener. The apostles, hesitant in their joy, ask one another, could it be he? The disciples at Emmaus take

---

[1] Acts 2:24. Hades or Sheol is the sojourn of the dead.

him for a traveler. Peter, John, and the others by the sea take him for a stranger who has strayed there by chance.

Thus, a kind of special training comes into being: the senses are no longer sufficient to recognize Christ.

Faith now becomes necessary: so long as they doubt, the apostles can establish no real contact with the risen One.

Hope becomes necessary: only when hope springs anew in the heart of the two disciples at Emmaus are they ready to understand the meaning of the breaking of the bread.

A sense of being loved becomes necessary: it is only when Jesus softly calls her by name, "Mary!" that all at once the Magdalene at last "hears" his voice and throws herself at his feet. It is "he whom Jesus loved" who senses his presence before everyone else by the shore of the lake and says to Peter, "It is the Lord!"

Another thing forces itself upon our attention: as soon as Christ is recognized, he disappears. It is useless to try to keep him back. Resurrection is not merely the resumption of the former life, like putting on a discarded garment again. "My little children," he said in sum at the last supper, "I am going away." Something reaches its final completion with Christ's death and resurrection.

Little children, yet for a little while I shall be with you. You will seek me and, as I said to the Jews, so I say to you: where I go you cannot come. [Jn 13:33]

Simon Peter intervenes, but Christ insists:

"Lord, where are you going?"
Jesus answered, "Where I am going you cannot follow me now; but you will follow later." [Jn 36]

On Easter Day Jesus tells the Magdalene: "Do not hold me thus"—for she has thrown herself at his feet—"but go to seek my brethren and tell them: 'I ascend to my Father and your Father, to my God and your God' " (Jn 20:17).

This is what Christ's resurrection inaugurates, this is what the sacrifice of Jesus has accomplished: he has risen as the firstborn. A new world begins with him.

However, during these forty days he communicates to them a sense of his continuous presence. He sends them to Galilee; and there, round every bend of the road, by the lake or in a house, while they think of him or speak of him or speak of Gospel episodes and discover a fresh meaning in them, or even while they are distracted and busy with other things, they suddenly come upon him and recognize him, since he is ever there, even before they have sensed his nearness.

These forty days are a whole pedagogy, a complete education in the new kind of presence of the risen Christ, who will proclaim in the end: "Behold, I am with you all days, even to the consummation of the world" (Mt 28:20).

Christ's Temptations and His Glory

At Djebel Karantal Jesus was tempted.

One might say that the very object of the three temptations finds its correspondence as well as its contrast in the forty days of Christ's glory.

In the desert Christ fasted and was hungry. Accordingly, in the Gospel we have frequent mention of the repasts of the risen Christ.

The two disciples at Emmaus recognize the Lord as he blesses and breaks bread (Lk 24:30-31). In the afternoon of Easter Day, one of the first things the risen Christ asks the eleven and their friends is, "Have you anything here to eat?" (Lk 24:41). By the lake the repast is more remarkable still: Jesus himself has lit a

fire of coals and roasted some fish, and presently he tells the
apostles, "Come and eat" (Jn 21:12). Just think of the joyous
intimacy, the convivial mood of this meal! Finally, while the
eleven are at table, he again manifests himself "during a meal
that he shares with them" (Acts 1:4, Mk 16:14) before he leads
them to Mount Olivet for the ascension.

The disciples have mastered his teaching on fasting; they now
share their meals with their risen Lord.[2] Christ now leaves his
Church a repast as a supreme act of religion and a bond of
brotherhood among themselves. Each time the last supper is again
commemorated, the risen Lord will again come personally to his
own. "Do this in remembrance of me. . . . For as often as you
will eat this bread and drink the cup, you proclaim the death of
the Lord until he comes" (1 Cor 11:24, 26).

This sharing of meals with Christ from the last supper until
the ascension initiated the Church into the reality expressed in
the Canon of the Mass soon after the Consecration:

Wherefore, O Lord, remembering the blessed passion of this same
Christ, your Son and Our Lord, his resurrection from the dead, and
his glorious ascension into heaven. . . .

In the second temptation Satan suggested that Christ throw
himself from the pinnacle of the Temple. The angels, he said,
would carry Jesus in their hands. Now, at the end of these forty
days of glory:

[Jesus] led the eleven toward Bethany, and he lifted up his hands and
blessed them. [Lk 24:50]

And when he had said this, he was lifted up before their eyes, and a
cloud took him out of their sight. [Acts 1:9]

[2] Acts 10:41. The apostles "have eaten and drunk with Christ" after
his Resurrection.

[He] was taken up into heaven, and sits at the right hand of God. [Mk 16:19]

Commenting on the mystery of the ascension, St. Paul raises a prayer that God, "the Father of glory," will

. . . enlighten the eyes of your mind, so that you may see . . . the exceeding greatness of his power toward us who believe.

Its measure is the working of his power, which he has shown in the person of Christ in raising him from the dead, and setting him at his right hand in heaven above every Principality and Power and Virtue and Domination. . . .

And all things he has made subject under his feet. . . . [Eph 1:17-22]

What a contrast between the distorted triumph of a human messianic undertaking such as the demon had suggested and the unique grandeur of God's designs as revealed in the Lord's ascension at the end of the forty days of glory!

In the third temptation, the devil offered Jesus all the kingdoms of the earth if Jesus would but worship him.

During the forty days of fulfillment, Christ converses with his friends about the Kingdom of God. To Pilate he has already declared that his Kingdom is not of this world, that his power is "not from hence." Ordering Peter in the Garden of Olives to put away his sword, he added: "Or do you suppose that I cannot entreat the Father and he will, even now, furnish me with more than twelve legions of angels?"[3] (Mt 26:53). And now he gives his Church her commission:

All power in heaven and on earth has been given me. Go, therefore, and make disciples of all nations, baptizing them in the name of the Father and of the Son and of the Holy Spirit. . . . [Mt 28:18-19]

[3] See also Pt 3:22.

Such is his Kingdom, a Kingdom of disciples, a Kingdom of the children of God. And this Kingdom which he gathers here below will be finally and permanently established by him, the true Josue, in the true Land of Promise. The twenty-fourth psalm, used in the Liturgy of the entrance into the sanctuary, expresses this mystery of Christ the king, entering heaven:

Be lifted up, O gates, be lifted up, O eternal gates: let the King of glory enter in!

Who is this king of glory?

The Lord, strong and valiant: Everlasting, the Lord of hosts. [Ps 24:7–8]

Another psalm proclaims the universal kingship of Christ and serves as a basis for the liturgical prayers of Ascension Day and the Sunday within its octave. The memory of this third temptation in the desert lends emphasis to this psalm, which celebrates the sanctity of Christ ascending into heaven.

God ascends in the midst of acclamations. . . .

For God is the king of all the earth; sing wisely!

God reigns over all the nations; he sits on his throne of sanctity.

The princes of the peoples are gathered together with the People of the God of Abraham. To God belongs the armor of the earth: He is exceedingly exalted. [Ps 47:6, 8–10]

JESUS' PREPARATION OF HIS CHURCH

Jesus prepares his Qahal, the People of his choice, his Church. Such is the second significant feature of the period that follows his resurrection.

On Easter Day begins the task of *gathering together* all those whom his passion has scattered.[4] When the disciples at Emmaus come back to Jerusalem in the evening of this day, they find "gathered together the eleven and their companions" (Lk 24:33).

Jesus calls his disciples to meet him in Galilee (Mt 28:7), and according to St. Paul, on one occasion Christ appears to more than five hundred brethren (1 Cor 15:6).

The apostles have been chosen "under the inspiration of the Holy Spirit," and it is to them that Christ imparts his instructions; it is to them that, in various ways, he shows himself alive after his death. It is they whom he introduces into the mysteries of the Kingdom of God (Acts 1:2-3). They are the "witnesses of the resurrection" (Acts 1:22).

Christ equips them for their mission by giving them the power to baptize (Mt 28:19). The mystery of the Jordan is thus extended to all the waters of baptism, as is the mystery of the Red Sea—the People of Israel were baptized "in Moses," while the Church is baptized "in Jesus." He also gives them the power to forgive sins (Jn 20:22-23), extending his own power to them. He has already given them his own body and blood (Mt 26:26-28).

He now sends them forth:

As the Father has sent me, I also send you. [Jn 20:21]

Going into the whole world, preach the good tidings to every creature. [Mk 16:15]

Before the day appointed for the descent of the Holy Ghost, the apostles select someone to replace Judas and thus restore their original number (Acts 1:21-26).

And Peter, after his triple denial during the days of the passion, is invited to make a triple protestation of love: "Peter do you love me?" "Yes, Lord, you know that I love you." Then Peter is

[4] "Then all the disciples left him and fled" (Mt 26:56).

confirmed as universal shepherd: "Feed my lambs. . . . Feed my sheep" (Jn 21:15-17).

The body of the Church is now fashioned, and there is nothing further to do before sending into it the breath of the Spirit so that on Pentecost Day the Church, the holy Church of the Word made flesh, may finally make her debut.

TEACHINGS ON THE KINGDOM

". . . for forty days [he spoke] of the Kingdom of God" (Acts 1:3). This teaching on the Kingdom appears as one of Christ's most important activities during the glorified period that closes his life on earth.

Clarifications

What does this final teaching of Christ consist in? First of all, in reminders.

Regarding the incident of Jesus' purifying the Temple by driving out the vendors and his speech about the sanctuary destroyed and rebuilt in three days, John observes:

But he was speaking of the temple of his body.

When, accordingly, he had risen from the dead, his disciples remembered that he said this, and they believed the Scripture and the word that Jesus had spoken. [Jn 2:21-22]

After the Transfiguration: ". . . as they were coming down from the mountain, Jesus cautioned them, saying: 'Tell the vision to no one until the Son of man has risen from the dead'" (Mt 17:9).

On Easter morning the dazzling angels of the sepulcher ask the women come to anoint the body of Jesus, "Why do you seek the living one among the dead? He is not here. He is risen. Remember how he spoke to you . . ." (Lk 24:5-6).

Very often in the three years of Christ's public life, the apostles have not understood their Master's teachings, but during these forty days of association with the risen Christ they grasp the hidden meaning of the Gospel episodes by thinking them over again.

Commentaries on the Scriptures

Most important of all Christ's teaching after the Resurrection is his instructions on the Scriptures, which will become the foundation of the apostles' theology. He teaches them to refer the events, the words, and the mysteries of the Gospel to the foreshadowings and doctrine in the Old Testament.

St. Luke describes the journey of the risen Christ, in the semblance of a traveler, with the two disciples to Emmaus. One of them explains the reason for their profound sadness and gives the unknown traveler what can be considered the first life history of Jesus, a history that ends with the failure of his death. The stranger then asks:

"O foolish ones and slow of heart to believe in all that the prophets have spoken! Did not Christ have to suffer these things before entering into his glory?"

And beginning with Moses and with all the prophets, he interpreted to them in all the Scriptures the things referring to himself. [Lk 24:25-27]

Christ speaks of Moses (the Law), of the prophets, and of all the Scriptures. He explains them and relates them to himself, making the mystery of his passion and glory the center around which they revolve.

These are the words which I spoke to you while I was yet with you, that all things must be fulfilled that are written in the Law of Moses and the prophets and the Psalms concerning me. [Lk 24:44]

St. Luke continues to emphasize this point, and what he says with such forcefulness remains for all time the central fact of the whole Christian faith:

Then he opened their minds that they might understand the Scriptures, and told them: "Thus it is written that the Christ should suffer and should rise again from the dead on the third day; and that repentance and remission of sins should be preached in his name to all nations, beginning with Jerusalem." [Lk 24:45–47]

With this the Gospel suddenly assumes immense proportions that neither the apostles nor the disciples had ever guessed before.

Moses

THE LAMB OF GOD

Andrew and John remember a phrase of the Baptist, their old teacher, when he pointed out Jesus to them. Seeing Jesus coming toward him, he exclaimed: "Behold the Lamb of God who takes away the sins of the world" (Jn 1:29). The words set them thinking, and they followed this man. But now when they think of the Pasch, of the lamb which it was an obligation to eat with great solemnity and whose blood was a sign before God (Ex 12:1–4), they recollect that Jesus himself said with ominous significance: "You know that after two days the Pasch will be here, and the Son of man will be delivered up to be crucified" (Mt 26:2).

And to think that they celebrated this Pasch together with him!

They also recall Abraham's words to his son as the two of them climbed Mount Moriya.[5] Isaac asked: "I can see the fire and the wood, but where is the lamb for the sacrifice?" And Abraham, in his faith, replied: "God will provide a lamb, my son" (Gn 22:7–8).

They remember, finally, an astonishing prophecy about a lamb that carries the sins of the world (Is 53:4–5). Nobody knew who this lamb might be, but all Israel was familiar with the prophecy and awaiting its fulfillment.

John, above all, meditates upon these mysteries and keeps them in his heart. He will tell us in his Gospel all that he learns during these forty days: "For God so loved the world that he gave his only-begotten Son; that those who believe in him may not perish, but may have life everlasting" (Jn 3:16).

Peter, too, commenting on the Pasch, speaks of "the precious blood of Christ, as of a lamb without blemish and without spot, foreknown before the foundation of the world but manifested in these last times for you" (1 Pt 1:20).

THE BRAZEN SERPENT

Christ alluded to another image: the brazen serpent. The Israelites, as a punishment for their insubordination, were stung by venomous serpents. To save them Moses installed a brazen serpent on top of a pillar, as Everlasting instructed; and anyone bitten by any snake who looked at the brazen serpent recovered (Nm 21:6–9). Biblical tradition preserved this incident. Now listen to Jesus:

And as Moses lifted up the serpent in the desert, even so must the Son of man be lifted up, that those who believe in him may not perish, but may have life everlasting. [Jn 3:15]

[5] The hill of the Temple, only a few steps from Calvary.

The disciples have heard, of course, but as usual they have not understood. Jesus reminds them of this sign and then interprets it: "When you have lifted up the Son of man, then you will know that I Am"[6] (Jn 8:28).

"Lifted up"—what does this mean? "And I, if I be lifted up from the earth, I will draw all things to myself" (Jn 12:32). And John sees again in memory the cross of Jesus.[7] Didn't everybody on that day look upon Jesus raised on a pillar? The apostle understands now, and once more in his Gospel will explain the meaning of Christ's reference to the brazen serpent: "Now he said this signifying by what death he was to die" (Jn 12:33).

At the end of the forty days, John can once again see Christ lifted up in his glory.

ABEL'S SACRIFICE

Toward the closing of his great day in the Temple, Jesus, alluding to the murder of Abel (that very ancient tradition of the suffering just man), said: ". . . upon you will come all the just blood that has been shed on earth, from the blood of Abel the just . . ." (Mt 23:35).

The apostles remember this day very distinctly; they remember how tense the atmosphere was. They recall above all the frightful cry, three days afterwards, hurled this time against Jesus himself, bound and standing before Pilate: "His blood be on us and on our children!" (Mt 27:25).

Genesis, Exodus, the Book of Numbers—all foreshadow Christ! And Jesus said as much:

[6] "I Am" in the same sense that God gave to his name when he said to Moses, "I am Who Am" (Ex 3:14).

[7] "And he who saw it has borne witness . . ." (Jn 19:35).

"Abraham, your father, rejoiced that he was to see my day. He saw it and was glad."

The Jews therefore said to him: "You are not yet fifty years old, and have you seen Abraham?"

Jesus said to them: "Amen, amen, I say to you, before Abraham came to be, I Am." [Jn 8:56–58]

And the apostles remember how the Jews took up stones to kill him; he was forced to disappear from sight.

Now they are enlightened by their risen Lord, and the meaning of all these things dawns on them at last. The whole of the Pentateuch announced Christ.

You search the Scriptures. . . . And it is they that bear witness to me. . . .

For if you believed Moses, you would believe me too, for he wrote of me.

But if you do not believe his writings, how will you believe my words? [Jn 5:39, 46–47]

Scripture is but one. The mystery it reveals is one, too: Christ in his Passover.

To fathom the divine depths of recent events—so very recent; perhaps a week, a fortnight, a month old—the apostles turn to the whole of tradition and Scripture: Moses, the Prophets, and the Psalms, as Jesus said. The Old Testament is divided into these parts, or perhaps we might say into the Law, the Prophets, and the Scripture.

The Prophets

Let us examine the sign of Jonas, who is here called "The prophet."

Some of the scribes and Pharisees said to Jesus, "Master, we would like to see a sign from you" (Mt 12:38).

It sounded like a challenging demand. Jesus never accepted this kind of demand, and here replied that no sign would be given them except the sign of Jonas the prophet. Then he went on to mention the three days and three nights he would spend in the seclusion of the tomb.[8]

Then there was the unexpected reference made before the Sanhedrin of his People to Daniel's prophecy. This prophecy, chronologically the last, was well known to everybody. The high priest had tendered to Christ a solemn oath:

"I adjure you by the living God that you tell us whether you are the Christ, the Son of God."

Jesus said to him: "You have said it. Nevertheless, I say to you, hereafter you will see the Son of man sitting at the right hand of the Power and coming upon the clouds of heaven." [Mt 26:63–64]

This was an enormity! The high priest tore his garments and exclaimed: "He has blasphemed; what further need have we of witnesses? There, you have yourselves heard the blasphemy!" (Mt 27:65).

Yes, what Jesus said was an enormity: he placed himself at the very center of eschatology and posed as the mysterious Son of man, wafted upon the clouds up to the Ancient of Days, up to the very throne of God![9]

But now that he has conquered death, now that the risen One converses with his apostles, can they be astonished any longer? Very soon they will watch him rising above the clouds of heaven, and the angels will inform them, "This Jesus who has been taken

[8] See pp. 65.
[9] See Dn 7:13.

158

up to heaven will come in the same way as you have seen him going up to heaven" (Acts 1:11).

And re-examining the old prophecies, Christ explains to the apostles what they say concerning him.

Here we must pause and study chapters 52 and 53 of Isaias. These are the most astonishing pages in all the Old Testament and some of the most sublime in the whole Bible.

During the Babylonian Exile, the People no longer had sacrifices since these could be offered only in the Temple of Jerusalem, but they came together, nonetheless, in the assemblies called synagogues where they read and explained the Scriptures and prayed the psalms.

But one day, between six and five centuries before Christ, an unknown prophet inspired by the Holy Spirit appeared and began a long series of prophecies about a mysterious servant of God who was to come. One of these prophecies especially, the fourth in the series, announced an extraordinary thing, so extraordinary that the kings themselves and the nations would be astonished: this servant of God would be unjustly judged, trampled upon, and finally killed; but his suffering, freely and voluntarily accepted in loving submission, would become the means of men's redemption.

The problem of suffering and death presented itself with special insistence to the exiles. Later on, Job would try to give a partial solution to it, but this prophecy offers no explanation. The just one, according to the prophecy, merely meets sorrow and takes it upon himself, thus relieving others who also carry its burden. And specifically because he offers his life as a sacrifice, the just one will live on and triumph after death. This servant will actually be a conqueror.

But who is he? No one knows. The prophecy has been studied over and over again, century after century.[10] The very history of the People of Israel, humiliated, oppressed, enslaved, can be read in it. The hope was thus born that this People would have a glorious future. But the prophecy is quite personal; the death foretold, especially, is that of an individual person. Who is he?

It is precisely this that Jesus explains to his friends during the forty days. To do so, obviously, he needs simply to make them recollect the events of his life, the great week of the passion, so fresh still in their memory.

In the first stanza of the prophecy, it is God who speaks:

Behold, my servant will succeed! He will be exalted, and extolled, and will be exceeding high.

As many have been astonished—his face will be inglorious among men, and his form among the sons of Adam—

so will he astonish many nations: kings will stay shut-mouthed before him, for they will see that which nobody had yet told them, that which they had never heard before. [Is 52:13–15]

"Exalted"—the apostles have seen the cross "exalted" on Calvary! On it they have seen Christ, disfigured, bleeding, crowned with thorns—a frightful sight! John remembers the words: "And I, if I be lifted up from the earth, will draw all things to myself" (Jn 12:32). Jesus said this on Palm Sunday, a few days before the crucifixion. And now his glory is just as astounding: nations and kings will witness it. In a few days, in full view of his friends, the risen Christ will ascend to heaven. Surely the two exaltations or liftings are closely connected with each other.

[10] Witness the Ethiopian who goes back home from Jerusalem, where he has gone for the Pasch. What is he reading in his chariot? Isaias 53:7–8. He asks Philip the Deacon, "Of whom is the prophet saying this?" And Philip, explaining this text, tells him about Jesus (Acts 8:32–35).

Jesus perhaps tells them also of this prophecy by Isaias: "On that day the root of Jesse will stand up as an ensign for the nations; the Gentiles will seek him, and his sepulcher will be glorious" (Is 11:10).

In the second stanza of Isaias' servant poem, a group, astonished by this prophecy, comments upon it as in the choruses of ancient times:

Who could believe what we have just heard? And to whom has the arm of Everlasting been revealed?

He has grown up as a tender plant before him and as a root out of a thirsty ground. There is no beauty in him, nor comeliness, and no sightliness that we should be desirous of him:

despised and the most neglected of men; a man of sorrows and acquainted with suffering; like one before whom we cover our face;[11] he was despised and we took no notice of him. [Is 53:1–3]

It is true. This prophecy did not originate in the heart of man; it sprang from the heart of God.

The apostles remember the conversation that worried them so in Caesarea Philippi, near the frontier of Israel, when Jesus inquired, "Who do men say the Son of man is?" "You are the Christ, the Son of the living God," Peter replied (Mt 16:13, 16). And Jesus called him "blessed!" It was very rare for Jesus to be able to praise his apostles. But Christ took this opportunity to add the thing that so terribly upset them: it was necessary, he said, that the Son of Man suffer much in Jerusalem, even that he be put to death. How shocked they all were, even though the announcement had been followed immediately by the promise of his resurrection!

[11] That is, a leper.

But now that Christ's words have been fulfilled, they are struck by this prophecy: a man of sorrows, of all sorrows; and deserted, too—yes, they themselves, the apostles, all of them, ran away. "I do not know this man," Peter insisted with an oath. Jesus was left completely to himself. And he was despised—people spat upon him, slapped his face, and insulted him. "He saved others; himself he cannot save," they jeered (Mt 27:42).

Stripped of his garments, he seemed like a leper on the cross. John saw him with his own eyes, and the others had it from hearsay. And wasn't it all foretold?

In the third stanza of Isaias' prophecy, the chorus is heard again, unfolding the new revelation of the theology of suffering:

And yet, it was our infirmities that he was carrying, and our sorrows that weighed upon him. We have thought of him as of one chastised, as one struck by God and afflicted.

But he was wounded for our iniquities; he was bruised for our sins. He was chastised for the sake of our peace, and by his bruises we are healed.

All we like sheep have gone astray; everyone has turned aside into his own way. And Everlasting has laid upon him the iniquities of us all. [Is 53:4–6]

The apostles can now fathom the mystery of the passion, and their hearts break. In their sorrow and wonderment, their souls swell up with gratitude and fear, with joy and love: *our* sorrows, *our* sufferings, *our* sins, *our* chastisement have fallen upon him! How well they understand the mystery of the Redemption as they examine his wounds and touch his side! "My Lord and my God!" (Jn 20:28).

In the fourth stanza, the prophet speaks in a monologue, and here the lamb of God comes in:

Ill-treated, he has submitted, and has opened not his mouth. He has been led as a lamb to the slaughter, and as a dumb sheep before the shearer.

He has been seized by force and judgment, and who was there to defend his cause? He has been erased from the land of the living. For the wickedness of his people he has been struck.

They have placed his tomb among those of the ungodly, and in his death he has been placed with the rich. . . . [Is 53:7–9a]

Was this, then, what the Baptist meant when he called Jesus the Lamb of God? And that astonishing silence during the whole night of his arrest, when the various charges were brought up against him, how noble it appears now! "Do you make no reply? What are these charges brought against you?" But he kept his silence and made no answer to the high priest (Mk 14:60–61, Mt 26:62–63). Herod, too, asked him several questions, but there was no answer from Jesus (Lk 23:9). "Do you make no reply? See how many charges they bring against you." But Jesus did not reply, and Pilate was greatly surprised (Mk 15:4–5, Mt 27:12–14). "Where do you come from?" Pilate asked then; and Jesus' silence remaining unbroken, he continued: "Do you not know that I have the power to release you or to crucify you?" To this Christ replied: "You would have no power at all were it not given you from above" (Jn 19:9–11).

Who stood up for him? Anyone?

The false witnesses were there, of course.

He was condemned. Caiphas, Annas, Herod, Pilate, all condemned him: blasphemer, fool, agitator. . . .

For our sins he was put to death. And the apostles remember also the tomb of Joseph of Arimathea. The tomb, too, is mentioned in this prophecy made six centuries ago but which sounds as if it were a few days old.

In the fifth stanza the prophet continues his monologue: this death, he says, is a religious sacrifice, and the just one will live:

And yet he has done no iniquity, nor was there untruth in his mouth.

But Everlasting was pleased to bruise him, to subject him to suffering; if he lays down his life as a sacrifice of expiation, he will see a long-lived seed, and the will of Everlasting will prosper with him.

Because his soul has labored, he will see light and be filled. [Is 53:9–11a]

Even Jesus' enemies have rendered homage to his truthfulness: "Master, we know that you are truthful and you care naught for any man, for you do not regard the person of man but teach the way of God in truth" (Mk 12:14).

"This is my beloved Son, in whom I am well pleased," the Father said at Christ's baptism in the Jordan. Christ's sufferings, too, then, must be pleasing to God. But it is in the resurrection that the Father's joy "will prosper with him:"

For this reason the Father loves me: because I lay down my life that I may take it up again.

No one takes it from me, but I lay it down of myself. [Jn 10:17–18]

All the mysterious sayings of the Gospel are finally explained as Christ comments during the forty days on this prophecy of the servant.

The account of the last supper throws full light upon this fifth stanza: ". . . if he lays down his life as a sacrifice of expiation." "This is my body," delivered for us, he said; "This is my blood of the new Covenant;" "Take and eat" (Mt 26:26–28). Haven't they in fact sat down and eaten this body?

"Father," he added, "I thank you because it has pleased you to reveal these things to the little ones." The little ones are the

apostles, who now learn from a glorified Christ about the wisdom
and the love of the Father.

The closing verse of the Isaias stanza explodes like a skyrocket
of joy: ". . . he will see light and be filled." This light was as
bright as lightning on Easter Day (Mt 28:3), and it still beams
out softly every time the Lord appears to them. "For . . . in your
light we see the light" (Ps 36:10). The light of the resurrection
has enlightened everything.

In the sixth and last stanza of the Isaias prophecy, the speaker
is again God:

This just one, my servant, will teach justice to the multitudes, and he
will bear their iniquities.

Therefore will I assign to him many people, and he will divide the
spoils with the strong, because he has delivered his soul unto death
and was numbered among the wicked, and he has borne the sins of
many and has prayed for the transgressors. [Is 53:11b–12][12]

The just one has become our justification. The apostles are
already beginning to see the signs of the final victory predicted
by this stanza. "Go, therefore, and make disciples of all nations"
(Mt 28:19), Jesus has told them. "All power . . . has been given
to me" (Mt 28:18). We already have a glimpse of the vision of the
Apocalypse in which we are told of all that will be accomplished
by the Church under the action of the Holy Spirit:

After this I saw a great multitude which no man could number, out
of all nations and tribes and peoples and tongues, standing before the
throne and before the Lamb, clothed in white robes and with palms
in their hands.

And they cried with a loud voice, saying: "Salvation belongs to our
God, who sits upon the throne, and to the Lamb." . . .

[12] The rendering of this poem of the servant differs somewhat from
that of the Bible of Jerusalem.

These . . . have washed their robes and made them white in the blood of the Lamb." [Ap 7:9–10, 14b]

This great passage in Isaias has affected the disciples deeply. The Gospels, Acts, Epistles, and Apocalypse will use this prophecy as a reference point.

What shall we say to these things? If God is with us, who is against us?

He who has not spared even his own Son, but has delivered him for us all, how can he fail to grant us also all things with him? [Rom 8:31–32]

The Psalms

Among the messianic psalms, the sixty-ninth gives us the prayer and lament of the man who founders in the mire and is surrounded by countless enemies. His prayer is heard by God, and the psalm ends with humble and joyful thanksgiving.

Several verses are like advance clarion calls of Gospel episodes, especially the passion: ". . . I looked for compassion, and I found none; for consolers, and there was none. . . . And . . . in my thirst, they gave me vinegar to drink" (Ps 69:21–22).[13]

Peter refers specifically to this psalm when, at the end of the forty glorious days, even before the descent of the Holy Ghost, he explains in the Cenacle the treason of Judas (Acts 1:16–22): "let their dwelling be devastated, and let there be none to dwell in their tents" (Ps 69:26; Acts 1:20). Where has Peter learned these things, who during the public life of Jesus seems so little versed in the Scriptures?

Peter and Paul discover a prophecy of the resurrection also in Psalm 16.[14] This psalm is a reconfirmation of faith in the one

13 See also vv. 5b and 10.
14 See Acts 2:26–28 and 13:35.

true God and of loyalty to the Covenant. The whole of Israel is portrayed as a nation of Levites, that is, server of the true religion.

Everlasting is the portion of my inheritance and my cup: it is you who will restore my inheritance to me.

The boundary lines mark for me an enclosure of delights: my inheritance is goodly to me. [Ps 16:5–6]

Particularly significant are the verses in which the man who has chosen God for his portion is certain that even after death he will not be separated from God. He sees a path leading to life, a fullness of joy beyond the portals of death. This is a great discovery, an unexpected foreknowledge, a grace given to the People of Israel, relatively unenlightened about the mysteries of heaven and resurrection:

Therefore, my heart and my soul have been glad, and my flesh will rest in safety, because you will not leave my soul in Sheol, nor will you allow your friend to see the tomb.

You will teach me the path of life before your face, fullness of joy at your right hand, and eternal delights. [Ps 16:9–11]

If this is what is in store for God's friend, for the faithful member of God's People, how much more glorious must be the destiny of the Holy One!

Psalm 22, closely related to Isaias 53, is one of the most explicit biblical passages on the mystery of the passion of Jesus. The first words of this psalm were uttered by Christ on the cross: "My God, my God, why have you forsaken me?"

But I am a worm and no man, the reproach of men and the outcast of the people.

All they that see me laugh me to scorn; they sneer at me and wag their heads:

"He hoped in Everlasting: let him deliver him now, since he is his friend!" [Ps 22:7–9]

Down to the last detail, this is what happened in the passion.

They have dug my hands and feet; I can count all my bones. These people watch me and stare at me; they part my garments among themselves, and upon my vesture they cast lots. [Ps 22:18–19]

The Messiah enters into the prayers of the poor; he makes it his own prayer, for he sees their distress. But he also praises their confident jubilation.

All the ends of the earth will remember and will be converted to Everlasting; and all the kindreds of the Gentiles will adore in his sight.

For Everlasting is a king, and the master of the nations. . . .

My soul will live for him, and my race will serve him. Everlasting will be exalted to the future generations, and his justice to peoples not yet born. . . . [Ps 22:28–32]

This psalm throws a little light on the depths of the soul of Christ nailed to the cross.

Psalm 2 contains another great messianic prophecy which the apostles discover during these forty days. On it they base their first Church prayer while Peter and John are in prison (Acts 4:25–28).

Why are the Gentiles in a rage, and the nations in this vain uprising?

The kings of the earth stand up, and the princes conspire against Everlasting and his anointed one [Christ]. [Ps 2:1–2]

It is the decree of Everlasting that bestows on his Son the Kingdom of all the nations of the earth. If the risen Christ brings this psalm to the notice of the apostles, they must be filled with awe when they discover the mysterious meaning which some of the verses take on:

I will announce the decree of Everlasting. He has said to me: "You are my son; this day have I begotten you.

"Ask me, and I will give you the Gentiles for your inheritance, the uttermost parts of the earth for your possession." [Ps 2:7–8]

Among the messianic psalms, Psalm 110 recurs with particular frequency in the Gospels, the Acts, and the Epistles.[15]

This psalm tells us of God, in his wisdom, performing the investiture of the King-Messiah, consecrating him a priest for all eternity, and making him sit at his right hand. Jesus on one occasion challenged his enemies by reminding them of this placement: "How then does David in the Spirit call him Lord . . . ? If David, therefore, calls him Lord, how is he his son?" (Mt 22:42, 45).

St. Peter quotes these same words on Pentecost in the first sermon ever preached in the history of the Church. Once again, where and when has Peter learned this interpretation? It can only be during these forty days.

Everlasting said to my Lord: "Sit at my right hand. . . ."
The scepter of your power, Everlasting, will extend to Sion. . . .

"With you is the principality in the day of your birth, upon the holy hills, from the womb, in the dawn of your youth."

Everlasting has sworn and he will not repent: "You are a priest forever according to the order of Melchisedech." [Ps 110:1–4]

[15] This is the first psalm of Sunday Vespers.

Matthew, Peter, Paul in the Epistle to the Hebrews[16]—these are surely important witnesses. Psalm 110 introduces us to the mystery of Christ the king and priest.

During the instructions of Jesus' teachings of these forty days, the apostles acquire complete certitude about one fact: the death of Christ has not been a matter of chance or coincidence; it was decreed by God. After Pentecost, when the apostles begin themselves to bear witness to Jesus, they insist most strongly on this.

Him, when delivered up by the settled purpose and foreknowledge of God, you have crucified and slain by the hands of wicked men.

But God has raised him up, delivering him from the sorrows of Hades, because it was not possible that he should be held fast by them. [Acts 2:23–24]

Addressing the people, Peter adds:

And now, brethren, I know that you acted in ignorance, as did also your rulers.

But in this way God fulfilled what he had announced beforehand by the mouth of all the prophets, namely, that his Christ should suffer. [Acts 3:17–18]

Here Peter contrasts human ignorance with God's designs—he has mastered at last the lore of the Scriptures!

In their first prayer, these early Christians assembled together declare that Herod and Pilate, together with the heathen nations and the People of Israel, have only done "what you, in your power and wisdom, had decreed to be done" (Acts 4:28). The same view recurs in Paul's and Peter's writings (1 Cor

---

[16] Mt. 22:42–45; 1 Pt 3:33; Heb 1:13, 5:6.

15:3–4; 1 Pt 1:10–11). Obviously the theme is a familiar one in the apostles' preaching.

God knows beforehand (these, of course, are human words, and therefore inadequate in relation to God) all the evil and all the sins of men, who will torture Jesus in his passion and put him to death. God wills, however, that his beloved Son accept all this and thereby redeem the world and establish the Kingdom of saints.

In keeping with the repeated periods of forty days and the forty years in the desert, all of which either prepared or renewed the mystery of the Covenant, the forty glorious days of the risen Christ perfect the preparation of his Church. These days fall under the influence and are illuminated by the light of the risen Savior. The infant Church must possess the most complete conviction of her Lord's victory. She is born only when Christ, having completed his work, ascends into Heaven.

The Qahal, the People of Jesus Christ, are therefore essentially eschatological, that is, an institution orientated toward the end of the world and the beginning of eternity: the Church simultaneously envisions Christ tempted and Christ triumphant.

She will herself re-enact this mystery in her life.

To sustain her faith and stimulate her hope, she reads the Scriptures, in which she continually discovers, with ever-new astonishment, "the breadth and length, the height and depth . . . [of] the love of Christ that surpasses all knowledge . . ." (Eph 3:18–19).

[May] the God of Our Lord Jesus Christ, the Father of glory, grant you the spirit of wisdom and revelation to acquire a deep knowledge of him!

[May] he enlighten the eyes of your mind, so that you may see the hope that his calling opens out to you, the glorious riches in his inheritance among the saints, and the exceeding greatness of his power toward us who believe.

Its measure is the working of his power, which he has shown in the person of Christ in raising him from the dead, and setting him at his right hand in heaven. . . .

And all things he has made subject under his feet, and has given him as head over all the Church, which indeed is his own body. . . . [Eph 1:17–20, 22–23]

The Church's Lent

SACRED history moves on. The liturgy leads us to live the events of our salvation today. Lent extends the mystery of Christ's forty days in the desert to the members of the Church.

As we have seen, between Christ's baptism in the Jordan with its divine manifestation and Christ's conflict with the devil's temptations there is a close and intentional connection, as is emphasized in the Gospels. The Church's Lent is placed in exactly the same context.

THE DEVIL

The attack that the devil made against the Head of the body is now being made against the members.

And the dragon was angered at the woman [a glorious woman with the sun for a garment, the stars as a crown, and the moon as a foot rest, whose Child has been "caught up to God"], and went away to wage war with the rest[1] of her offspring who keep the commandments of God and hold fast to the testimony of Jesus. [Ap. 12:17]

This is why the Church, beginning on the very first Sunday in Lent, proposes for our consideration the temptation and victory of Christ. She returns to the theme of the devil on the third Sunday (Lk 11:14–28), and continues this exercise of Christian ascesis and prayer throughout the forty days. On the vigil of Easter, strengthened by the power Christ has communi-

---

[1] The "rest" of the offspring of this woman—who is both the Church and the Virgin Mary—are the Christians.

cated to her, she reaches a climax in her liturgy with the solemn renunciation of Satan, the profession of faith in the Trinity, and the celebration of baptism or the renewal of its promises.

She then enjoins on all the faithful the recitation of the prayer that Jesus himself has taught her. The Our Father contains seven requests, all of them related to the forty days of Christ in the desert:

> Our Father, who art in heaven,
>
> Hallowed by thy name [thou, who hast revealed thyself at Jesus' baptism].
>
> Thy Kingdom come [the Kingdom Christ will announce after the sojourn in the desert].
>
> Thy will be done on earth as it is in heaven [thy will from which Christ would not let himself be separated by temptation].
>
> Give us this day our daily bread [when we hunger after thee, on our way to thee],
>
> and forgive us our trespasses as we forgive them that trespass against us [for we, too, are sinners!],
>
> and lead us not into temptation [but lend us the strength of Jesus],
>
> but deliver us from the Evil One [who has been vanquished by Our Lord].
>
> Amen.

THE DESERT

The setting for Lent is the desert.

During Lent the Church creates a desert for her children. She denudes her liturgy of all pomp, flowers, and alleluias, intensifying this atmosphere of austerity in Passion Week.

Lent is also a closed season to the solemn celebration of marriage.

In the hymn of the night office of these forty days, the Church requests her children to be "more moderate in words, food, sleep, and recreation."

Christians, consecrated to the mystery of Christ, are a people set apart, dedicated to the redemption of the world. As such, they are called upon to participate in some measure in the life of their Lord in the desert.

FASTING

Ash Wednesday, the opening day of Lent, is a day of fast. No amount of reasoning and no appeal to "progress" can ever obscure the fact that Christ, emerging from the waters of baptism, went to the desert to fast. What the Head has done, the members also must do. Adapted to our bodily weakness and recommended by the Church to our individual fervor, fasting must remain in our lives.

Blow the trumpet in Sion, proclaim a fast, call a solemn assembly, gather the People. . . .

And rend your hearts and not your garments, and turn to Everlasting, your God, for he is gracious and merciful, slow to anger and rich in grace. . . . [Jl 2:15–16, 13]

This passage from the prophet Joel, read daily from Ash Wednesday onward, characterizes the spirit of Lent. Christians appear as one body. What Christ has done as an individual we will do *as a Church*. Our fast will be not the result of a famine or a punishment inflicted upon us, but the spontaneous outcome of love of God, sorrow of heart, and charity among brethren; it will be a liturgy.

It is our hearts that God wants to purify and sanctify.

Fasting is conceived as a direct means to that interior renewal and spiritual vitality toward which the prophets of old guided the People of Israel, especially after the Exile.

On the Friday after Ash Wednesday, the liturgy gives us a description of the hypocritical fast which is but a formality:

Behold, in the day of your fast you make your will be done and oppress your servants.

You fast in contention and strife and strike the poor with your fists. It is not such fasts as you observe today that will make your prayer heard above.

Is that a fast that pleases me: for a man to mortify his body? or to hang his head like a reed? or to lie prone on sackcloth and ashes? Will you call that a fast day acceptable to Everlasting? [Is 58:3–5]

It is plain to see what the prophet as a spiritual instructor condemns here; true fasting must be accompanied by a change of heart:

Is this not rather the fast that I like, the command of Everlasting, the Lord? Break asunder unjust chains, untie the ropes of the yoke; let them that are oppressed go free, and break down every yoke.

Share your bread with the hungry, and shelter the homeless poor. Clothe the naked, and do not ignore one of your own flesh.

Then will your light break out like the dawn, and your own wound will be quickly healed. Your justice will go before your face, and the glory of Everlasting will follow after you.

Then will you pray, and Everlasting will hear your petitions and answer: "Here I am." . . . do away with the yoke and the threatening gesture and wicked desire.

. . . share your bread with the hungry and feed him who is oppressed . . . . [Is 58:6–10]

This, then, is the road the Church embarks on: fast and charitableness, self-sacrifice and generosity. One is reminded of the evangelical works of mercy and the parable of the last judgment (Mt 24:40).

Christ himself takes up this prophetic teaching on the value of the fast that is pleasing to God, and speaks of delicacy and reserve in the invisible presence of God: "But you, when you fast, anoint your head and wash your face so that your fast may be known not by men but by God, who is there in secret; and your Father who sees in secret will reward you."[2]

This point is of such importance in the eyes of the Church that she stresses it unceasingly in her prayers throughout Lent:

[May] these bodily penances become fruitful through the sincerity of our minds.[3]

That while abstaining from bodily nourishment, we may refrain as well from all dangerous pleasures.[4]

Sanctify, O Lord, through this sacrifice our Lenten penances, that what our observance expresses exteriorly, that may be achieved interiorly as well.[5]

. . . grant that those whom you command to abstain from bodily food may also refrain from pernicious vices.[6]

And this prayer so well links our penance with the holy and victorious fast of the Lord Jesus: ". . . may we find joy in your

[2] Mt 6:17–18. The liturgy introduces this passage in the Ash Wednesday mass.

[3] Collect of the mass for Friday after Ash Wednesday.

[4] Secret of the mass for the first Sunday in Lent

[5] Secret of the mass for Saturday of ember week in Lent.

[6] Collect of the mass for Wednesday of the second week in Lent. See also the collects of the masses for Friday and Saturday of the third week.

service, O almighty God, that by curbing our earthly attachments, we may more easily understand heavenly things."[7]

PRAYER

The abstention from bodily food during Lent demands, by contrast, an abundance of spiritual nourishment. Our hunger is above all a hunger for the word of God, which is a major theme of this period. During Lent the liturgy of the Church draws lavishly on the word of God. Each day has its own special mass: readings from the Old or the New Testament, meditational chants, appropriate and repeated prayers.

PSALM 91

On the first Sunday in Lent a whole psalm sustains the introit, the gradual and tract, the offertory, and the communion prayer.

Already mentioned in connection with the temptations of Christ,[8] this psalm constitutes one of the most characteristic lenten prayers.

You who dwell in the shelter of the Most High[9] and abide in the shadow of the Mighty One,[10]

say to Everlasting: "You are my protector and refuge, my God, in whom I trust!"

He delivers you from the snare of the hunters who seek destruction.

He shelters you with his wings, and beneath his pinions you will find a refuge.

[7] Collect of the mass for Wednesday of the fourth week in Lent.
[8] See p. 136–137.
[9] "Most High," in the Hebrew text *Elyon*.
[10] "Mighty One," in the Hebrew text *Shaddai*.

You will not be afraid of the terrors of the night, nor the arrow that flies in the day,

nor the pestilence that lurks in the dark, nor the scourge of noontime.[11]

A thousand may fall at your side and ten thousand at your right hand, but you are out of reach, for his fidelity will be your armor and your shield.

But open your eyes, and you will see the reward of the wicked.

For you say: "Everlasting, my refuge," and make of the Most High your shelter.

No evil will come to you, nor will the plague approach your tent, for he has given his angels charge over you, to keep you in all your ways.

In their hands they will bear you up lest you dash your foot against a stone.

You will walk upon the lion and the asp; you will trample on the lion cub and the dragon.

Because he hoped in me I will deliver him; I will exalt him because he has known my name.

He cries to me and I answer him; I am with him in his tribulation, and I deliver him and glorify him.

I will fill him with length of days, and I will show him my salvation. [Ps 91]

This prayer of wisdom is laden with images of the desert, and tells us a great deal about the feelings, dispositions, and relationship with God of the People of Israel.

But it also relates to Christ during his forty days at Djebel Karantal. Jesus in the desert knows this psalm and prays it. The approaching devil tries to use it for his own ends, but the

---

[11] Some versions say here "the noontime devil."

prophecy it contains is fulfilled and Christ emerges as conqueror.[12]

The first strophe (vv. 1–2) is an act of complete confidence by the wise soul, the soul that has chosen God and trusts in him. We are in the desert—God is a shade against the sun; and we are exposed to our enemies—God is a fortress and a refuge.

The second strophe (vv. 3–4) shows us, on the one hand, the dangerous fowler plying his string. His aim is to kill; hence he suggests the destroyer, the devil. On the other hand we are shown God in the act of sheltering his own under his wings. This recalls Israel's coming to Sinai and its vocation:[13]

In a desert land he adopts [his People], in the dazzling solitude of the wilderness. He shelters them and teaches them, and keeps them as the pupil of his eye.

Like the eagle that watches its aerie and hovers above its young ones, so God spreads out his wings and takes them and carries them on his pinions. [Dt 32:10–11]

The third and forth strophes (vv. 5–6 and 7 with 4b) speak of the dangers of the night, of the day, and of the sultry noon[14]— the terrors of the night, the *surprises* of the night, as the Canticle puts it (Ct 3:8). When Judas leaves the Cenacle on Maundy Thursday, St. John briefly remarks: "Now it was night" (Jn 13:30). Night is the time for treason.

The arrow that flies by day signifies assault and war.

The scourge that sows devastation at noontime[15] is the con-

---

[12] See vv. 14–16.

[13] Jesus uses the same metaphor: "Jerusalem, Jerusalem . . . how often would I have gathered your children together, as a hen gathers her young under her wings . . ." (Mt 23:37).

[14] "Evening and morning and at noon I will lament, and he will hear me" (Ps 54:18).

[15] If we use the versions here that have "the noontime devil," we are referred once more to the temptations of Jesus.

tagion that smites and spreads and slays a thousand on one side, ten thousand on the other. One is reminded of the terrible pestilence during the reign of David:

Now it was the time of the harvest. And Everlasting sent a pestilence upon Israel from the morning until the time appointed, and there died of the people from Dan to Bersabee[16] seventy thousand men.[17] [2 S 24:15]

In the face of these calamities the psalm preserves a serene confidence: do not be afraid, for you are beyond the reach of danger! "His fidelity will be your armor and your shield." This throws considerable light on the narrative of Christ's temptations in the desert.

The fifth strophe (vv. 8–9) invites us, amid the vicissitudes of life and especially in difficult and trying times, to keep the end in sight: the day of retribution to the wicked. On one side are the sinners, those who take no notice of God; on the other, in direct opposition to them, are you who say, "Everlasting, my refuge," and make of him your shelter.

The sixth strophe (vv. 10–11) seems at first a reference to the plagues of Egypt that harmed only the persecutors. The People of God took to the road and were guided by God's angel throughout their journey in the desert. But here the image of this angel is, as it were, multiplied and extended to each individual member of Israel.

The seventh strophe (vv. 12–13) develops the theme of this angelic protection. Angels see to it that the unshod foot does not stumble over the stones strewn on the road, that vipers do not

[16] "From Dan to Bersabee" means the whole of Israel. Dan was the northern city, Bersabee the southern.

[17] The figures are exaggerated. The sense is that the scourge can slay in a short time a great number of people.

sting and wild animals do not harm. In the same strain Christ assures his disciples, "I have given you power to tread upon serpents and scorpions, and over all the might of the enemy, and nothing will hurt you" (Lk 10:19).

In the eighth strophe (vv. 14–16) we hear the voice of God himself making one final promise. He delivers and sets free, exalts and glorifies. He is present in times of distress and gives an answer to the soul that clings to him, knows his name and invokes it: "I will show him my salvation."

"All the ends of the earth will see the salvation of our God" we are told in Isaias' Book of Consolation (Is 52:10). And when old Simeon, the perfect type of the just one of the Old Testament, is moved by the Spirit and comes to the Temple to receive the infant Jesus in his arms, he exclaims:

Now you may dismiss your servant, O Lord, according to your word, in peace,

because my eyes have seen your salvation, which you have prepared before the face of all peoples:

a light to enlighten the Gentiles, and a glory for your People, Israel. [Lk 2:29–32]

It is good for us to take up the prayer of this psalm, to make it our own prayer, or better, to let it mold our spirit. This psalm is very appropriately recited at compline, during visits to the sick, and in exorcisms.

. . . you give us, O Lord, a desire to pray.[18]

O Everlasting, the God of my salvation, I pray to you by day and in the night I sigh before you; let my prayer fly up to you.[19]

[18] Prayer over the people of the mass for Monday of the fourth week in Lent.

[19] Ps 88:2–3, in the offertory of the mass for Saturday of ember week in Lent.

Blessed is the man . . . whose will is in the law of Everlasting, who meditates on his law day and night.[20]

. . . that this Lenten fast may be profitable to us, fill our minds with your divine doctrine.[21]

The two major features of the forty days of the Church, a period set aside each year for insistent supplication to and renewed contact with the Word of God, are fasting and prayer. These are her weapons against the tempter's wiles.

It is undoubtedly because of this that two other psalms recur so frequently in the liturgy of the Lenten Masses. The two are Psalms 19 and 119. They are both prayers whose object is meditation on and praise of the Law of God.

Psalm 19

In its second part (vv. 8–15), this psalm is a simple, elementary prayer of contemplation. A pious soul appears before God and lovingly tells him how holy his Law is, how well he has done all things, and what a happy portion it is to be in his service.

The law of Everlasting is perfect, a comfort to the soul; the testimony of Everlasting is truthful, giving wisdom to little ones.[22]

The precepts of the Lord are right, a joy to the heart; . . . sweeter than the honey and the honeycomb. . . . Therefore your servant keeps them.[23]

[20] Ps 1:2.

[21] Collect of the mass for Monday of the first week in Lent.

[22] V. 8, in the introit of the mass for Saturday of the second week in Lent.

[23] Vv. 9a, 11b, and 12a, in the offertory of the mass for the third Sunday in Lent.

Purify me, O Lord, of [my secret sins]. Save me, your servant, from pride; let it have no power over me. Then shall I be without spot and shall be cleansed of the greatest sin.[24]

Accept the whispered prayer that rises to you unceasingly from my heart, O Everlasting, my support and my redeemer.[25]

Almost all of this psalm is thus found spread through the various Lenten masses. This suggests that, together with Psalm 91, it ought to be a favorite Lenten prayer for us.

Psalm 119

In the Bible of Jerusalem this long, whispered prayer is entitled "Praise of God's Law," or sometimes "The Alphabet of Divine Love" because each verse begins with a different letter of the Hebrew alphabet. Bremond makes special mention of it in his *Literary History of the Religious Sentiment* because this psalm introduces us to the People of God's very intimate and practical manner of praying.

It is also a prayer in which the Church, during her Lenten recollection, sees herself portrayed, for she is today's Israel of God, the People of Jesus. Here are some select passages to be found in the missal.

Quicken me according to your promise, . . . and I shall understand your testimonies.[26]

[24] Vv. 13b–14, in the communion of the mass for Monday of the fourth week and the gradual of the mass for Tuesday of the third week in Lent.

[25] V. 15, in the introit of the mass for Friday of the fourth week in Lent.

[26] Vv. 154 and 125, in the offertory of the masses for Friday and Saturday after Ash Wednesday.

Open my eyes and I will consider the wondrous things of your law.
. . . Teach me your will; . . . give me understanding, and I will
learn your commandments.[27]

Your commandments have been my delight, and I have greatly loved
them. I lift up my hands to your commandments that I love.[28]

You have ordered your commandments to be observed faithfully.
Oh! may my ways be directed to fulfill your precepts![29]

Direct my steps according to your word, and let no iniquity have
power over me.[30]

Be bountiful to your servant, and I shall live: I shall keep your word;
. . . quicken me according to your word.[31]

The faithful Christian endeavors to understand better and
better the right observance of God's Law. He does so with
enthusiasm because he realizes that this Law brings life to his
soul. This study is not dictated by servile fear; it is rather a
labor of love, for "I lift up my hands to your commandments
that I love."

TODAY

On Passion Sunday, the refrain to the invitatory psalm[32] repeats with greater insistence than ever, ". . . today, may we hear
his voice: 'Harden not your hearts . . .'" (Ps 95:7-8).[32]

These words are addressed to everyone who is present. They

[27] Vv. 18, 26b, and 73b, in the offertory of the mass for Monday of the
first week in Lent.

[28] Vv. 47-48, in the offertory of the mass for Wednesday of ember
week and for the second Sunday in Lent.

[29] Vv. 4-5, in the communion of the mass for Thursday of the third
week in Lent.

[30] V. 133, in the offertory of the mass for Saturday of the third week
in Lent.

[31] Vv. 17 and 107b, in the offertory of the masses for Friday and Saturday of Passion Week.

[32] See p. 104.

are God's own words reminding us of Massah and Meribah, for the trial of the desert—a trial Christ himself went through—is today our own. We ourselves hear the voice of God, are delivered from Egyptian bondage, plunge into the waters of baptism, and march onward toward the true Land of Promise, our loins girt as befits pilgrims.[33] We also sojourn in the desert.

The events of salvation history reach down to us today, and the conditions of salvation are the same.

Therefore, as the Holy Spirit says: "Today, if you hear his voice, do not harden your hearts as in the Quarrel, on the day of temptation in the desert, where your fathers tried me, putting me to the test, when for forty years they had seen my works.

"Wherefore I was irritated by this generation, and I said: 'They always err in their hearts; they have not known my ways.' And I have sworn in my wrath: 'Never will they enter into my Rest.'" [Heb 3:7–11]

Such is St. Paul's comment in his Epistle to the Hebrews. And he adds:

Take heed, brethren, lest perhaps there be in any of you an evil, unbelieving heart that would turn away from the living God.

But exhort one another every day, while it is still today, that none of you be hardened by the deceitfulness of sin [Heb 3:12–13]

To win the battle *today,* "we have been made partakers of Christ" (Heb 3:14), who came to his victory as the Head of the body of which we are members. The People who were encamped in the Sinai could not enter into the Promised Land ("Never will they enter into my Rest"). And to show how the plan of God is unfolding and that every Christian has his place in it, St. Paul continues:

[33] 1 Pt 1:13, 2:12.

186

Since then it follows that some will enter into God's Rest, and they to whom it was first promised did not enter in because of their unbelief,

[God] appoints another day, which is our today, saying by David after so long a time, as quoted above, "Today, if you hear his voice, do not harden your hearts." [Heb 4:6–7]

Essentially this Epistle emphasizes the gripping pertinence of sacred liturgy. It is today, *now,* that God loves us, calls us, accosts us. And it is today that we reply to him and take up our position in his plan. Today is eternity!

The liturgy of Christmas brings this fact forcefully home to us. On the vigil of Christmas the introit of the mass alerts us by reannouncing the promise made to the People in the desert: "In the evening you will know that the Lord will come, and in the morning you will see his glory" (Ex 16:6–7). The introit of midnight mass echoes the Father's own words: "[Everlasting] has said to me: 'You are my son; this day have I begotten you' " (Ps 2:7).

In the solemn celebration of the last supper on Maundy Thursday evening, one word is daringly added to the prayer that leads up to the consecration of the bread: "Who [Christ], the day before he suffered for our salvation and that of all men, that is to say, today. . . ." The same word is added to the preface of the mass for Pentecost, in which the Church prays to the all-holy Father through Christ, Our Lord: "Who, ascending above all the heavens and sitting at your right hand, did send down today the promised Holy Spirit upon the children of adoption. . . ."

Thus, Lent brings us to see that we are truly living in the "today of God."[34]

[34] This is the title of a book by Prior Roger Schultz which appeared in the United States under the title, *Living Today for God.*

The Lenten liturgy evokes, one after the other, all the holy Lents of the past. On ember Wednesday, we read about Moses and Elias, as well as the episode of Jonas; on the following Saturday and on the second Sunday Moses and Elias are found together with Jesus on the Mountain of the Transfiguration. Then on Friday of the third week we are told of the water flowing from the rock as well as the episode of the Samaritan woman from St. John's Gospel. The fourth Sunday gives us an account of the multiplication of the loaves, a symbol of the manna. On Tuesday of the fourth week the Epistle is about the golden calf, while the Gospel reading is Jesus' discussion of Moses. On Monday of Passion Week, the narrative of the forty days of Jonas precedes St. John's Gospel on the living waters that Christ has given us.

When we finally come to the Easter vigil we find all these themes together, echoing each other—from the immolation of the lamb to the deliverance from Egyptian bondage in the Red Sea crossing, from the pillar of fire suggested by the Paschal candle to the blessing of the baptismal font:

O God, by purifying with the waters of the flood the sins of a guilty world, you have given us a foreshadowing of baptism. . . .

You open the font of baptism for the renewal of all mankind.

Far removed from this water, O Lord, be every unclean spirit at your command; far removed be all malice and snare of Satan. May his power never prevail upon it. Let him not encircle it, nor enter it by stealth, nor infest it with his deceit. . . .

I bless you, [water], likewise, through Jesus Christ who in the Jordan was baptized in you, who brought you forth from his side; who commanded his apostles that they baptize in you all believers, saying: "Go, teach all nations, and baptize them in the name of the Father and of the Son and of the Holy Ghost."

I bless you, O water, in the name of the true God who brought you forth from the rock to quench the thirst of his People.

Holding the Paschal candle, which symbolizes the Christ Light, the priest dips it into the water thrice, each time more deeply, as Jesus dipped into the Jordan, and says, "May the power of the Holy Ghost descend into the depths of this font."

Thus it is that the Lent of the Church fulfills all the past forty-day periods of the Bible.

At the end of her festal year, in the full light of the forty days of fulfillment, the Church is finally ready to utter her supreme prayer: "Come, Lord Jesus, come!"